D0722890

The Antitrust Laws

The Antitrust Laws

A Primer

Fourth Edition

John H. Shenefield
and
Irwin M. Stelzer

The AEI Press

Publisher for the American Enterprise Institute
WASHINGTON, D.C.

2001

Available in the United States from the AEI Press, c/o Publisher Resources Inc., 1224 Heil Quaker Blvd., P.O. Box 7001, La Vergne, TN 37086-7001. To order, call toll free 1-800-269-6267. Distributed outside the United States by arrangement with Eurospan, 3 Henrietta Street, London WC2E 8LU, England.

Library of Congress Cataloging-in-Publication Data

Shenefield, John H.
    The antitrust laws : a primer / John H. Shenefield and Irwin M. Stelzer.—4th ed.
      p. cm.
    Includes bibliographical references and index.
    ISBN 0-8447-4154-X (cloth: alk. paper)
    1. Antitrust law—United States.   I. Stelzer, Irwin M.
II. Title.
    KF1650.S53   2001
    343.73'0721—dc21   2001045088

1 3 5 7 9 10 8 6 4 2

The AEI Press
Publisher for the American Enterprise Institute
1150 17th Street, N.W., Washington, D.C. 20036

Printed in the United States of America

For Judy and Cita,
who made what we like to think was the
sacrifice of our company so that we
might unburden ourselves of this tract.

Contents

CONTENTS

CONTENTS

CONTENTS

Acknowledgments

Even so modest a volume benefited from the counsel of several colleagues. We especially thank Robert Bork and Christopher DeMuth for their comments. They nudged us as far as they could in the direction of accepting consumer welfare as the sole standard by which business conduct should be appraised under the antitrust laws. That we did not join their Chicago contingent is due more to our stubbornness and our own reading of the law and economics of antitrust than to any lack of advocacy skills on their part.

Alfred E. Kahn over the years has contributed much to the thinking of both of us. Scott Stempel and Donald Klawiter, careful practitioners that they are, made several helpful suggestions and corrections. Paul Rubin, Douglas Wetmore, and Douglas Leeds provided helpful detail at important points. John Wotton was kind enough to share his knowledge of international antitrust enforcement with us by reviewing chapter 12. Jeffrey Baines and John Terzaken assisted in the thorough updating reflected in this new edition.

ACKNOWLEDGMENTS

Jeanne Buster's accuracy made pulling the new text together much easier.

All those people were an enormous help. The book's shortcomings are our own.

The Antitrust Laws
A Primer

ONE
Introduction

Antitrust laws . . . are the Magna Carta of free enterprise. They are as important to the preservation of economic freedom and our free-enterprise system as the Bill of Rights is to the protection of our fundamental freedoms.

United States v. Topco Associates, Inc.,
405 U.S. 596, 610 (1972)

This book is intended to replace the businessman's fear and loathing of the antitrust laws with a basic understanding of what they are about and to acquaint students with these important legal and economic precepts. Properly understood, the Sherman, Clayton, and Federal Trade Commission Acts are a businessman's assurance that he will have the opportunity to compete fairly for all the business he can get and keep the rewards of his success. For consumers, those acts represent a regime designed to provide the widest choice of products at the lowest price.

The antitrust laws, in short, are a set of rules of the game meant to preserve the competitive process, to enable markets to direct resources to the uses that will

1

best satisfy consumers. By preserving the competitive integrity of markets, the laws make it unnecessary for the government to arrogate to itself the function of deciding what gets produced, where, and by whom. They make it unnecessary for the government to set prices. They make it unnecessary for the government to assign raw materials to this or that factory or to attempt to pick technological winners. In short, by preserving competition, the antitrust laws minimize government intervention in business affairs. That is the reason they are sometimes referred to as the "Magna Carta of free enterprise." It is only when competition is infeasible or has been throttled by government or private action that the long arm of government must replace the invisible hand of the market as the regulator of dealings among businesses and between businesses and consumers.

The several laws, court decisions, and enforcement agency policies that we describe in the following pages contain the rules of the competitive game. The Antitrust Division of the Department of Justice, the Federal Trade Commission, and, at times, the state attorneys general and lawyers for private plaintiffs watch closely for violations. The courts are the ultimate referees. Commercial enterprises are the players and consumers the beneficiaries, if the rules are observed and the contest hard fought.

It is not surprising that some of the players are at times more than mildly annoyed with a referee's calls. After all, such decisions often involve the application of judgment to complex sets of facts. But the individual decisions are less important than the policy they are designed to implement: that competition be fair, that there be no artificial barriers to deter entry into any business, that society's limited resources be efficiently used, and that consumers have available to them a wide range of competitively priced goods.

This book tries to convey the full texture of the antitrust laws: the meaning of the statutes, as applied by the enforcement agencies and interpreted by the courts, informed by modern economics. The book is, of course, no substitute for the advice of experienced counsel in specific situations and so, alas, is unlikely to reduce the bills about which it is so fashionable for businessmen to complain. But an appreciation of the broad purposes of antitrust policy, combined with a specific lay knowledge of the law, will, we hope, enable students to understand the interaction of law and economics in producing competition policy and equip businessmen who must live in the real world to react more wisely to day-to-day situations. Should you accept a competitor's invitation to a hotel room to discuss the ruinous price war that has wreaked havoc with this quarter's earnings? Should you accept an invitation to give a speech on that subject at your trade association's annual meeting? Can you merge with a leading competitor, the better to cope with foreign competition? And can an underperforming dealer be terminated? No, no, probably, and under certain circumstances. Those are the preliminary guidelines that will emerge from chapters 7, 8, and 9—guidelines that can inform the reader's judgment pending careful review by his counsel.

A word about style. We have no illusions: a description of the antitrust laws cannot be made acceptable bedtime reading, except perhaps for insomniacs seeking relief. But it can be made accessible to the interested nonlawyer. That we have tried to do by minimizing jargon, legal citations, and other foot-notes. We hope we have not sacrificed precision to readability or conveyed an impression that the law is more certain and predictable in application than is the case. And, if we have been fortunate enough to pique your interest in exploring the subject in more depth, you might find our suggestions for further reading (appendix D) and our notes helpful.

TWO

The Origins and Objectives
of Antitrust

The market economy is one of the great works of human history. Markets have existed in one form or another ever since one primitive man killed more prey than he could eat and another killed less. But the more advanced conception of the market economy, in which the energies and desires of individuals are harnessed to the public good, is of comparatively recent origin; still more recent is the almost universal triumph of the market economy over alternative forms of economic organization.

Philosophical Origins

The year 1776 produced, along with the Declaration of Independence, Adam Smith's *Wealth of Nations*. That first treatise of classical economics describes the rational economic man as minding only his own business but at the same time being "led by an invisible hand" to promote the larger interest of society. Alexander Pope put it more poetically:

> Thus God and Nature link'd the gen'ral frame,
> And bade Self-love and Social be the same.

More refined thinking about the market economy was the work of the great Enlightenment liberals, including John Locke and Jeremy Bentham, who believed that the private enterprise economy presupposed the need for private property. Those were ideals that eighteenth-century revolutionaries and nineteenth-century gentry and middle class all could support. Those values were enshrined in the great political documents of the eighteenth century—the Declaration of Independence, the U.S. Constitution, and the French Declaration of the Rights of Man. Just as civil liberties required that government's power over the individual be limited, capitalism likewise required that government be forced to respect private property. Emphasizing the freedom of the individual and skeptical of centralized power and planning, capitalism and constitutional democracy alike liberated energy and creativity that even the sharpest critics could not deny. In the Communist Manifesto, Karl Marx declared, "The bourgeoisie, during its rule of scarce 100 years, has created more massive and more colossal productive forces than have all preceding generations together."

Most critics of the market economy focus not upon the central idea of free enterprise but instead on its potential for abuse. Wealth is in fact unevenly distributed; consumer sovereignty implies a range of choice for every buyer that is sometimes illusory; monopoly can stand the concept of free enterprise on its head; private transactions, mutually agreeable to the parties, may impose costs on others. The wars and depressions of the first half of the twentieth century dimmed the

6

luster of the market economy. Mass unemployment and economic peril forced an expansion in the role of government and produced socialism, with its collective ownership of the means of production, and the welfare state.

Now, at the beginning of the twenty-first century, the socialist economies have largely collapsed. Just as the breach in the Berlin Wall signaled the end of communism as a political force, it also triggered the reemergence of the market economy as an ideal for developed and developing nations alike. History has taught us that the ills of free enterprise were not to be remedied by the suppression of individual initiative or abolition of the concept of private property. Rather, the key was to reestablish and reinvigorate the inherent strength of the market economy itself.

Historical Background

The engine of free enterprise is competition. When competition works, the market economy functions well. Numerous sellers, vying for customers, must produce goods and services of sufficient quality, and at acceptable prices, or be driven from the field. That necessity forces them to be efficient, to buy so-called inputs—labor and materials—at the lowest possible prices, and to use those inputs in such a way that total production costs are kept to a minimum.

But competition at times fails, for one of three reasons: either government, as a matter of policy, chooses to suppress it, for instance, by arrogating to itself the power to print money; or competition extinguishes itself, creating the need for government-imposed regulation, as for instance in parts of the electric utility industry; or private participants in the market subvert competition and thus prevent market forces from operating freely.

Where competition fails, government has two choices. It can either protect the consumer from market abuse by directly regulating the firm with monopoly power or restore the vigor of competition through antitrust enforcement that prevents competitors from conspiring to fix prices or individual firms from dominating markets.

Early precedents for government action to preserve a competitive marketplace, the focus of this primer, are to be found in the early English treatment of monopolistic practices. The reign of James I saw first a statutory, then a judicial, challenge to the royal monopoly grants, which came to be viewed as incompatible with the English Constitution. At the same time, judicial antipathy to private restraints that unnecessarily prevented or restricted the practice of a trade grew quickly. Various common law proscriptions of those trade restraints came across the ocean with the English settlers of the New World. But it was not until after the Civil War that Americans became truly anxious about the lack of effective tools to limit the abuse of monopoly.

As American business gained size, strength, and, in some cases, market dominance in the last half of the nineteenth century, opposition to monopolies likewise developed momentum as a political issue at both the federal and the state levels. The huge Standard Oil enterprise, closely followed by the sugar, whiskey, and other combinations, took the form of a trust—collecting shareholder voting power in the hands of a single managing trustee. Efforts to control those powerful interests were known as "antitrust" laws.

President Benjamin Harrison's 1889 call for "penal legislation" to control "dangerous conspiracies against the public good" resulted in the passage of the Sherman Act in 1890. That statute contains two fundamental provisions that still constitute the core of our antitrust laws. The first prohibited conspiracies in restraint of trade, and the second prohibited abusive practices aimed at gaining or keeping a monopoly. Neither, it should be noted, prohibited businesses from attaining huge size, so long as they did so merely by competing fairly. The legislation's lineage from its distant antecedents in the English common law was clearly recognizable.

Those who expected a period of vigorous enforcement following the enactment of the Sherman Act— and its many state law counterparts—were to be disappointed. Both enforcement authorities and courts were at first reluctant to apply the law as its framers had envisioned. For one thing, its meaning was not entirely clear: its drafters had chosen to forgo a detailed list of prohibited activities in favor of a generalized statute of constitutional breadth. As a result, even after successful prosecutions against the oil and tobacco trusts, pressure mounted for the enactment of further laws to strengthen the Sherman Act. After all three political parties—Democrats, Republicans, and Teddy Roosevelt's Bull Moose Party—came out in favor of more vigorous antimonopoly prohibitions in the 1912 campaign, two new antitrust statutes were enacted in 1914: the Clayton Act and the Federal Trade Commission Act.

The words of the antitrust statutes have remained relatively unchanged ever since, but their significance for the economy has varied greatly. Enforcement vigor has waxed and, sometimes, waned, particularly during the Great Depression when it was feared that falling prices were prolonging the depression, and the antitrust laws were therefore suspended for any industry that operated under a so-called code of fair competition. The only major additions to the statutory framework have been the Robinson-Patman Act, enacted in 1936 to deal with price discrimination, and the Celler-Kefauver Act, enacted in 1950 to invigorate the antimerger provisions of the Clayton Act.

The courts' interpretation of the antitrust statutes has evolved as the study of industrial organization and practices has changed our understanding of how markets work. In recent years economists have enriched antitrust analysis by developing tools that help to distinguish monopolistic from competitive market structures, and the behavior of monopolizing firms from those that are merely competing vigorously.

Those changing interpretations generate controversy. But the statutes and the central notion that competition is worth preserving remain generally accepted by all, regardless of political party or school of economic thought. Some quarrel with this or that decision; others seek modifications to accommodate what they perceive to be changes in the world economy. But almost all agree that the antitrust laws are of central significance to our economy. They do no less than establish the economic framework within which most Americans and their businesses operate.

Objectives of the Antitrust Laws

Stating the objectives of the antitrust laws is, surprisingly, no simple matter. The language of the statutes, the history of their enactment, and their subsequent interpretation by courts and commentators provide several major themes, but no unanimity. The precise definition of the goals of antitrust appears to depend on which antitrust statute is being analyzed, by whom, and for what purpose.

The Sherman Act, with its proscription of cartel and monopolizing behavior, seems to reflect most clearly the economic objective of enhancing consumer welfare by preventing practices that reduce competition. That pristine economic principle is also clearly reflected in the language of sections of the Clayton Act, in which various practices are condemned if their effect "may be substantially to lessen competition, or to tend to create a monopoly." Supreme Court decisions, both some of the earliest and some of the most recent, give full play to that economic objective. And in recent years, the weight of critical commentary, advanced in particular by the so-called Chicago School, even argues that the enhancement of consumer welfare is the exclusive goal of the antitrust laws' proscription of anticompetitive behavior.

But those views are hard to square with the historical background and the legislative history of the statutes. Supreme Court decisions over the years refer to a variety of antitrust goals. They point out that the early legislative debates also allude to social and political purposes of antitrust. No doubt some of the statutes, most notably the Robinson-Patman Act, were clearly motivated by a purpose to protect the Jeffersonian model of small dealers and competitors, notwithstanding some possible costs to society in terms of reduced efficiency. More recently, producer rather than consumer welfare is emphasized by those seeking to permit cooperation among competitors to spur technological innovation.

Others view fairness within an economic framework as key; they ask why consumers should be favored over producers. Many emphasize our society's abiding concern for the diffusion of private power and maximum opportunities for individual enterprise. That wider range of factors, in addition to consumer welfare, simply cannot be ignored without turning away from what has historically, and politically, been one of the central motivating factors behind the enactment, the acceptance, and the enforcement of the antitrust laws.

How then are those sometimes confusing and frequently conflicting objectives to be reconciled by enforcers and courts, not to speak of businessmen who seek to plan a lawful course of conduct? Begin by recognizing that the conflict between the economic and political objectives of antitrust policy is less serious in practice than in the abstract. Prevention of the accumulation of monopoly power contributes to consumer welfare by preventing price gouging; it also meets the sociopolitical objective of dispersing economic power.

It must be conceded, however, that conflicts between the social goals of antitrust policy (dispersed power and maximization of the role of individual entrepreneurs) and its economic objectives (consumer welfare and efficiency) have at times occurred. During the Great Depression, for example, the Supreme Court allowed some coal producers to eliminate competition among themselves to provide relief to a depressed industry, a social objective with no immediately discernible relationship to either economic efficiency or consumer welfare.

Where social and economic goals conflict, the economic goal must be presumed to have primacy. That emphasis is faithful to Adam Smith's notion that the "invisible hand" of competition should guide operation of the economy. Competition is, after all, the best means of eliminating excess profits; of allocating resources to their most efficient use; of forcing firms to produce goods of the highest quality at the lowest cost, in amounts consumers want; and of stimulating the generation and introduction of technological innovations. All those add to consumer welfare and, at the same time, effectively promote economic growth and prosperity, and the distribution of income in rough proportion to the value of individual contributions to the economy, all of which are the very definition of success for a national economy. To the extent that other objectives need to be served, such as small business protection, laws other than the antitrust laws serve those functions more efficiently and more precisely.

But establishing the primacy of economic efficiency as the goal of antitrust policy is often the beginning, not the end, of analysis. The problem of selecting the path to an efficient outcome remains. Should we forgo the short-term advantages of a possibly lethal price cut, announced by a dominant firm, in favor of the longer-run efficiencies that flow from maintaining multifirm rivalry? In short, must we on occasion protect competitors to preserve competition? Such protection may at times be nothing more than the costly coddling of the inefficient, and at other times a step necessary to maintain competition in the long run. Because economists cannot always provide clear guidance, and because political and social considerations cannot be ignored, especially in the face of such uncertainty, the courts face a sometimes difficult chore. But those cases, experience teaches, are rare. More often, the efficient solution is clear and not at war with society's noneconomic objectives.

Businessmen, faced with the daily need to make decisions that will avoid antitrust censure, must understand the rich and varied texture of those statutes as well as some of the key decisions the courts have made in applying them. The social and political goal is a system that reflects a sense of equity or fairness, that diffuses economic power, and that maximizes individual opportunity. The economic goal is to maximize efficiency and consumer welfare. Courts and prosecutors will surely focus most intensively on the economic goal, but the philosophical and historical underpinnings of the antitrust laws demand that they be sensitive to the noneconomic goals as well.

THREE

The Statutes

The process of understanding the antitrust laws must begin with the words of the statutes themselves. The oldest is the Sherman Act. Although it dates from 1890, it remains the core of the statutory regime. Every subsequent statute has been an effort to expand on or refine its provisions.

The Sherman Act

Section 1 of the Sherman Act proscribes agreements in restraint of trade. Congress had the choice of prohibiting a laundry list of specific activities that frequently constitute restraints of trade, such as price-fixing, bid-rigging, refusals to deal, and the like. Instead, it chose to proscribe restraints generally, in a provision of sweeping scope, to be developed and applied by the courts in specific cases.

The language of Section 1 provides that "every contract, combination in the form of trust or otherwise, or conspiracy, in restraint of trade or commerce among the several States, or with foreign nations, is . . . declared to be illegal." The trigger is a "contract," "combination," or "conspiracy." In the absence of some cooperative conduct or joint action involving at least two separate companies, that provision of the Sherman Act does not apply. The collective activity can involve two competitors, or a seller and its customer, or two buyers. The collective activity may be a secret conspiracy, or it may be a contract set down in black and white and approved by lawyers. The point is that, without the collective action, even if the conduct restrains trade in some sense, Section 1 cannot apply.

It is clear also from the language of the statute that the trade restrained must either be in or at least have an effect on interstate or foreign commerce. Two schoolboys who restrain the trade of baseball cards within a single school playground will not be covered by Section 1 because their activity is simply too trivial— too localized—in its economic impact. But the threshold is not high: a conspiracy to eliminate just one ophthalmological surgeon from the medical staff of a hospital that serves out-of-state patients comes within the reach of the statute.

Read literally, the words of Section 1 would prohibit all contracts or any other collective action that had the incidental effect of restraining trade regardless of the effect on competition or economic welfare. After all, every sales contract removes one buyer and one seller from the market for the duration of the contract and to that extent restrains trade. To get around that problem, the Supreme Court, in the 1911 *Standard Oil* case, sensibly interpreted Section 1 as prohibiting only restraints of trade that *unreasonably* restrict competition.

Over the years, as developed in specific situations in thousands of cases, the concept of unreasonableness has come to be analyzed in two different ways. First, there are restraints considered unreasonable per se, and therefore unlawful, without the need for elaborate inquiry into the factual context. Those restraints have been brought within the per se category only after the courts have concluded from past experience that they are manifestly anticompetitive and lack any redeeming virtue. Per se unlawful restraints include direct price-fixing or bid-rigging between competitors as well as the division of customers or markets.

"[T]here are certain agreements or practices which because of their pernicious effect on competition and lack of any redeeming virtue are conclusively presumed to be unreasonable."

NORTHERN PACIFIC RAILWAY V. UNITED STATES,
356 U.S. 1, 5 (1958)

Second, restraints are judged under the so-called rule of reason. For conduct not assigned to the per se category, antitrust analysis requires a weighing of the relevant circumstances to decide whether, on balance, the conduct is procompetitive or anticompetitive.

Like many other aspects of antitrust policy, that distinction between conduct that is a per se violation of the law and conduct that must be reviewed pursuant to the rule of reason is not a bright line. Some practices, while subjected to what the courts call per se treatment, nevertheless are evaluated by reference to market circumstances, including the extent of market power present and the substantiality of their effect on competition. Others are condemned outright, without any such further analysis. But those latter instances are increasingly rare. In recent years the rule of reason has been applied in an increasingly large number of

17

Section 1 cases. That does not mean, however, that the courts will examine the reasonableness of a price agreed to by competitors in a smoke-filled hotel room. But when confronted with agreements by competitors to exclude a rival from a trade association, for instance, the courts are increasingly likely to apply a "quick look" rule of reason and examine a few telling facts, such as whether the alleged restraint will inevitably restrict output or raise prices.

Beyond that truncated rule-of-reason analysis is a more amorphous category of conduct that is certainly not per se unreasonable and is neither on its face a restriction of output nor supported by market power. Consequently, it is subject to the full-dress rule-of-reason analysis that seeks to discover the actual competitive effect. Such full-dress rule-of-reason cases are naturally complicated and expensive; they frequently require the use of expert witnesses and intricate economic and statistical studies to help the court decide the net competitive impact of conduct in a particular industry.

Section 2 of the Sherman Act prohibits monopoly abuse. It states:

> Every person who shall monopolize, or attempt to monopolize, or combine or conspire with any other person or persons, to monopolize any part of the trade or commerce among the several States, or with foreign nations, shall be deemed guilty of a felony.

As with Section 1, Congress did not provide a list of objectionable acts or conduct. It preferred, instead, the sweep of general language and left it to lawyers and judges to elaborate the general principles in specific cases. Note, too, that the offense is monopolization, not monopoly. Whatever its applicability many years ago, the oft-heard "bigness is badness" slogan no longer has any relevance in antitrust enforcement. In short, the section condemns not sheer size, but abusive conduct by a monopolist, or unilateral or collective efforts to engage in exclusionary or predatory conduct to obtain monopoly status. High market share that results from efficiency remains unobjectionable; an identical share, obtained by systematic conduct designed to harm competitors, is likely to arouse the interest of the enforcement agencies.

Those, then, are the two provisions of the statute whose wide-ranging purposes were so succinctly summarized in *Northern Pacific Railway v. United States:*

> The Sherman Act was designed to be a comprehensive charter of economic liberty aimed at preserving free and unfettered competition as the rule of trade. It rests on the premise that the unrestrained interaction of competitive forces will yield the best allocation of our economic resources, at the lowest prices, of the highest quality and the greatest material progress, while at the same time providing an environment conducive to the preservation of our democratic, political and social institutions. But even were that premise open to question the policy unequivocally laid down by the Act is competition.

As befits a "comprehensive charter," the language of the Sherman Act is simple and general, and its scope is therefore limited only by the logic and self-discipline of the judges who interpret it: "The prohibitions of the Sherman Act were not stated in terms of precision or crystal clarity and the Act itself does not define them. In consequence of the vagueness of its language . . . the courts have been left to give content to the statute" *Apex Hosiery Co. v. Leader,* 310 U.S. 469, 489 (1940)). The Sherman Act continues to develop as new cases are brought and decided. Thus, the courts have the flexibility to respond to changing market conditions and to new economic learning about the nature and workings of the competitive process.

When antitrust enforcement was seen to have gotten off to a slow start, in the early days of the twentieth century, the nation's political leaders saw a need for further statutory enactments. The view of a majority of legislators and of President Woodrow Wilson was that the Sherman Act failed in two regards. First, it did not nip threats to competition in their incipiency—an elaborate way of complaining that antitrust law as it stood in 1914 locked the barn door after the horse was stolen. Second, the Sherman Act was seen as excessively general: what was thought to be needed was prohibition of specific practices that were likely to have anticompetitive effects.

The Clayton Act

One product of that pressure was the Clayton Act. The Clayton Act prohibited conduct that constituted not an accomplished trade restraint, as with the Sherman Act, but that might do so in the future. Thus, the statute focuses on conduct, the effect of which "may be substantially to lessen competition, or to tend to create a monopoly in any line of commerce." Reaching anticompetitive conduct "in its incipiency," the Clayton Act nevertheless requires a reasonable probability— not the mere theoretical possibility—that the conduct challenged would, if undisturbed, mature into a restraint of trade.

Section 2 of the Clayton Act, which was amended and replaced by Section 1 of the Robinson-Patman Act (enacted in 1936), makes it unlawful for any business engaged in interstate or foreign commerce to discriminate in price between different purchasers of the same type and quality of commodity, if the effect of the discrimination "may be substantially to lessen competition or tend to create a monopoly in any line of commerce, or to injure, destroy, or prevent competition with any person who either grants or knowingly receives the benefit of such discrimination, or with customers of either of them." But a price difference is generally permitted if it is carefully cost-justified or if the lower price is necessary to compete for the custom of a particular purchaser.

Other provisions of Section 2 of the Clayton Act prohibit the payment of certain kinds of commissions, brokerage fees, or other compensation, or the discriminatory provision of promotional or advertising allowances that are not offered on equivalent terms to other competing purchasers. Finally, Section 2 prohibits the knowing inducement or receipt of a discriminatory price prohibited by the act.

Section 3 of the Clayton Act prohibits certain kinds of agreements, known variously as exclusive dealing or tying, in which a product is sold only on the condition that the purchaser will not deal in the goods of a competitor of the seller. That section also applies only where the effect of the arrangement "may be to substantially lessen competition or tend to create a monopoly in any line of commerce."

Section 7 of the Clayton Act prohibits certain acquisitions by one business of another, whether by way of stock or assets purchase. Section 7 is also keyed to a substantial lessening of competition or the tendency to create a monopoly. While the language is not necessarily limited to the acquisition of a competitor, those are the acquisitions that can easily have the requisite anticompetitive effect, and they are the most often challenged.

The unifying principle of the Clayton Act provisions is that they look to the future and require a prediction of probable anticompetitive effect. The congressional thinking in 1914 was that remedies under the Sherman Act, requiring a finding of accomplished restraints of trade or monopolization, frequently came too late. Because the health of the marketplace hangs in the balance, the Clayton Act was Congress's attempt to fashion preventive medicine.

The Federal Trade Commission Act

Congress also enacted the Federal Trade Commission Act in 1914. It establishes an independent regulatory agency—the Federal Trade Commission—and gives it the power to (1) enforce the Clayton Act and the Robinson-Patman Act (but not the Sherman Act), and (2) challenge, in the words of the Supreme Court, "an unfair competitive practice even though the practice does not infringe either the letter or the spirit of the antitrust laws." Thus, the reach of the operative provision of the Federal Trade Commission Act—Section 5—is at least as broad as the Sherman, Clayton, and Robinson-Patman Acts combined. How much broader Section 5 may be is still a matter of controversy. To some extent, therefore, the Federal Trade Commission Act represents a duplicative, or complementary, enforcement regime, depending on one's viewpoint. The FTC's merger enforcement program is an example of powers complementing those of the Justice Department in a relatively efficient fashion.

As amended in 1938 by the Wheeler-Lea Amendments, the Federal Trade Commission Act now also prohibits unfair or deceptive acts or practices, whether or not they constitute "unfair methods of competition." The act is thus the centerpiece of the federal consumer protection regime. In addition, the FTC enforces a variety of other consumer protection statutes, including the Truth-in-Lending Act, the Fair Credit Reporting Act, and the Fair Packaging and Labeling Act.

Generally, the FTC's practical power to test the frontiers of the law by proscribing unfair methods of competition has focused on acts or practices that, although not violating either the Sherman or Clayton Act in a technical sense, nevertheless seem to violate the policies of those statutes. Although the statutory grant of power is somewhat open-ended, appellate decisions have limited the commission's jurisdiction, at least in the competition area, to conduct that is at least close, if not identical, to that already prohibited under the other antitrust laws.

FOUR

The Institutions and Procedures

The antitrust laws can be enforced in four different ways. First, the Antitrust Division of the Department of Justice may bring either a civil case to prohibit further violations of the law or a criminal case that can result in fines for businesses and jail terms and fines for individuals. Second, the Federal Trade Commission, which can bring civil cases for violations of certain antitrust statutes, but not criminal cases, works mainly through an administrative process of cease and desist orders and may insist on civil penalties or monetary consumer redress. Third, state attorneys general, in addition to enforcing state antitrust laws, can in certain circumstances bring civil lawsuits under the federal antitrust laws for injunctions against further violations and for damages. Finally, a private party that believes that it has been damaged by a violation of the antitrust laws can sue in federal court for an injunction to prohibit any recurrence of the violation and, more important, for treble damages, that is, an amount equal to three times the damage suffered by the plaintiff as the result of the antitrust violation.

Both the Department of Justice and the Federal Trade Commission have a variety of roles in antitrust enforcement and competition policy in addition to prosecuting violations. Each has an advisory opinion procedure that permits any business to inquire whether a contemplated activity is acceptable under the antitrust laws. Each on occasion has published elaborate guidelines that give quite specific direction on how particular commercial arrangements, such as mergers, licensing of intellectual property, foreign business conduct, or practices in the health care field, will be analyzed. Each engages in competition advocacy, so that in proceedings before government agencies such as the Securities and Exchange Commission or the Federal Communications Commission the regulators are forced to hear strong arguments in favor of a procompetitive position.

That administrative activity is the most accurate guide to what the agencies are planning and thinking. All those opinions, guidelines, and competition advocacy filings must be carefully reviewed to understand fully the policy positions and enforcement postures of the Justice Department and the FTC. And there is more. Consent decrees and consent agreements—those pleadings that settle government antitrust cases without any formal judicial findings—are significant events; the complaints that initiate antitrust cases may contain novel theories or new economic perspectives that provide insights into current antitrust enforcement policies. And like every government agency, the FTC and the Antitrust Division issue statements and press releases; their leadership finds occasions to give numerous, frequently revealing speeches to lawyers or to industry groups. All those sources, in addition to the case law and the words of the statutes themselves, form part of current antitrust jurisprudence. No antitrust lawyer dares to drop out of touch with any significant portion of that imposing body of subterranean law—if he does, his clients either will be missing a profitable step or will be in for an unpleasant surprise.

Picking Targets

In choosing cases to prosecute, each agency has the power to investigate by compelling the production of documents or testimony. The investigative phase will reveal with substantial precision the context, and therefore the competitive significance, of the conduct at issue. In deciding whether to sue, the agency will often have the benefit of explanations or arguments presented by the party whose conduct may be challenged. Business people and their lawyers frequently use that opportunity to be sure that the agency fully understands the relevant facts, and, for its part, the agency welcomes those exchanges. Such meetings take place initially at the junior staff level with the younger lawyers who are actually engaged in the investigation. At later stages there is the opportunity for additional meetings with supervisory personnel and, perhaps, with the political appointees in charge of the agency.

Such meetings are more than casual chats: those involved should prepare for them with as much care as they would prepare for trial. Facts must be marshaled and well presented; informal requests for more data should be honored promptly; speeches about legal generalities are to be avoided. Because those preliminary exchanges often prove fruitful, because agency budgets are limited, and because investigation separates wheat from chaff, the hundreds of leads, tips, and transactions brought to agency attention in a single year actually result in relatively few formal agency proceedings in court.

Criminal Prosecutions

The Antitrust Division has the option of prosecuting Sherman Act violations criminally and frequently does so with respect to those identified as per se unlawful. In addition, the division uses other criminal statutes—including those dealing with wire and mail fraud, false claims, perjury, and obstruction of justice—in its antitrust enforcement efforts. The division will seek to impanel a grand jury to investigate reliable information indicating the existence of criminal violations. Generally, the division receives that information from disgruntled former employees or from customers who note peculiar and improbable pricing patterns. In an increasingly important category of cases, the division receives such information even from a company that discovers on its own that it has been involved in culpable conduct and decides to take advantage of the division's policy of leniency in those cases in which a company reveals a violation and then cooperates fully in the subsequent investigation.

If criminal prosecution is pursued, the full weight of the criminal process is brought to bear. The Federal Bureau of Investigation or special investigators from other federal agencies may be employed, with their expert methods of criminal detection, investigation, and surveillance, and if indictments are eventually sought, arrest may follow. Convictions will lead to hefty fines, and for the individuals who were most culpable, certain jail time.

Going to Court

The Antitrust Division, the state attorneys general, and the private plaintiffs who choose to bring suit eventually find themselves before a federal court, where they attempt to persuade either a judge or jury of the correctness of their position. Those cases then take on the procedural trappings of large commercial litigation, replete with teams of lawyers and expert witnesses, extensive document discovery, dozens of witness depositions, often lengthy pretrial preparation followed by an extended trial, and then perhaps several years in the federal appellate process. Because of the Speedy Trial Act, the division's criminal prosecutions are somewhat more accelerated, but even there the investigative phase may last more than a year.

For its part, the FTC brings its cases before an administrative law judge, with procedures quite similar to federal court litigation, or in certain circumstances, directly in federal court. Both kinds of FTC cases may ultimately be appealed to a federal appellate court.

Because the antitrust statutes are framed in general terms, the enforcement agencies and the courts exert a powerful influence over the direction in which the law develops. Unless the agencies (or private parties) choose to bring suit, the courts are never presented with occasions to elaborate the statutes' commands in specific factual settings. Defendants, by settling, have the option to withdraw that opportunity from the courts even after suit is filed.

The courts themselves must be guided by the statutes, their legislative history, the precedents that other court cases represent, and authoritative commentary. The process of evolution is necessarily both gradual and incremental and thus gives the antitrust law a predictability precious to business people, who must invest in and plan for the future. Business people—assisted by their lawyers—can survey the body of relevant law, assess its applicability to particular conduct or practices, and, in most cases, come to rather precise conclusions about legal significance. As a result, the enforcement agencies often say that the private bar is the first line of defense to protect business people from straying unawares into violation of the law.

Settlements

Given the time commitment and the resources required for lengthy litigation, defendants frequently attempt to settle. In the case of mergers, defendants may eliminate certain features of the transaction that the Antitrust Division or the Federal Trade Commission finds anticompetitive. For example, the acquired company may have one division that competes with the acquirer; that division can be spun off.

In the case of conduct that the FTC or the Antitrust Division believes violates the law, the potential defendant can agree to cease or to modify its practices. And it can settle with private plaintiffs seeking damages by paying some compromise sum.

Settlement of criminal proceedings is more difficult, although there are stages in the criminal process where a plea bargain can be considered. The federal *Sentencing Guidelines* have reduced the flexibility that the Antitrust Division once had in such negotiations, but plea bargains are still routinely sought and negotiated, although very large fines and jail may be the price of a deal.

FIVE

The Analytical Framework: Markets and Market Power

With the exception of a few of the per se restraints, suspicious conduct is analyzed under the antitrust laws to determine whether it will produce injury to competition. Such a determination necessarily involves delineating the arena in which competition is occurring, known in the trade as defining the relevant market. After all, if the point of the exercise is to determine the effect of some business practice on competition, then the competitive reality must be isolated and analyzed. Firms compete to sell goods to a buyer; the buyer decides which mix of product, price, and quality best suits it. A restraint that is said to affect that interaction among buyers and sellers can be assessed only when all relevant buyers and sellers are identified. A relevant market consists of all buyers and sellers of all products that are actual or potential competitors with one another.

The objective of defining a relevant market is to determine the boundaries within which effective competition occurs, or, conversely, market power is exer-

cised. Put slightly differently, the aim of market definition is to determine what group of competitors could
jointly effect a substantial, durable price increase. For
such a determination to be made, several dimensions
of the competitive arena must be delineated.

First, the product involved in the competitive battle
must be identified: is it tin can versus tin can or tin can
versus all containers? Is the fight between natural gas
from different fields or among all fuels? Do championship boxing matches compete for paying fans and
television viewers only with other championship fights
or with routine boxing matches or with other sporting
events? Second, we must locate the boundaries of the
arena, its geographic dimension: is the fight between
domestic contestants only, or are foreigners battling
for the consumer's favor?

The Product Market

Courts attempt to include in the relevant market all
goods that consumers view as realistic substitutes, one
for the other. All goods or services that consumers
actually substitute for one another are, of course, in
the market. So, too, are products to which consumers
can readily switch, if the price of the product they are
using begins to rise sharply. A rise in transcontinental
air fares is unlikely to cause people to switch to trains;
a rise in New York–Washington shuttle fares well
might. So the market for transportation services would
in the first instance exclude rail, but in the latter case
include it. The test is at what point consumers react to
price rises by switching from one good or service to
another. Of course, not *every* customer will be willing
to switch brands or find alternatives when prices are
raised. It is sufficient that enough customers be willing

to make such substitutions to affect the conduct of sellers in the market. The courts are, in other words, interested in competition at the margin, in the presence of a significant number of customers for whom there are realistic substitutes for any firm's product.

The Geographic Market

In addition to defining the product dimension of the market, it is necessary to determine its geographic limit. A bakery in Manhattan produces the same bread as a bakery in San Francisco, but there is no sense in which they are competitive—transportation costs are prohibitive. By contrast, a manufacturer of jumbo jets in the United States is competitive with another manufacturer in Europe.

Market definition must take account of both realities. In the first case, the geographic markets are extremely local, perhaps occupying a small portion of Manhattan or San Francisco, respectively. In the case of jumbo jets, the geographic market is very likely worldwide. Again, the focus is on what alternatives are realistically available to the buyer.

The Competitors

After defining the product and geographic markets, we can identify the firms competing in those markets: all firms that supply that product or that could do so with relative ease. In the short run that would include all firms with the ability to supply that product by using the same personnel and equipment. In the longer term it would include all firms with the ultimate ability to shift from the supply of one good to another by adding some new equipment or new personnel.

That, then, is the hypothetical market within which the competitive effect of the conduct at issue can most realistically be analyzed—the analytical tool that best enables antitrust analysts to answer the crucial question: does the practice injure competition?

Market Power

Following the definition of the market, the next analytical step is to determine whether the conduct in question is carried out by a firm or group of firms with market power. Since the basic inquiry concerns competitive injury, which is usually defined as an artificial increase in price, restriction of output, or exclusion of competition, the sensible question is whether the firm or firms could possibly produce such an effect. In the absence of direct evidence of actual control over price or output, antitrust analysis tests for market power, which is viewed as the "surrogate for detrimental effects" (*Federal Trade Commission v. Indiana Federation of Dentists*, 476 U.S. 447 (1986)).

A shorthand way of assessing market power is to examine the market shares of the firms engaged in the suspect conduct. Market share is sometimes reckoned in simple percentage terms and at other times in somewhat more complicated ways. The effort, however, remains the same: to find out how much of all the business done by firms in the market is controlled by those said to be involved in the restraint of trade. Below some point, the firms' efforts even in the pursuit of nefarious purposes are viewed as harmless; above that point, as market share increases, the conduct takes on an ever more sinister significance.

For instance, mergers between two competitors, assessed within the defined market, begin to raise questions in the minds of antitrust enforcers when the combination obtains a significant market share, say, 20 percent of a market comprising many competitors. Two firms that agree to boycott a third may be guilty of an antitrust violation if together they constitute 70 percent of the relevant market. If their share is trivial, though, and the buyer has dozens of other sources, the agreement is of no competitive effect and cannot satisfy the competitive injury requirement of the antitrust laws. In that way, market share helps to reveal the potential for competitive injury.

Market share is, however, only one aspect of the analysis of market structure, albeit the most important one. Courts consider, too, whether high market shares have persisted over time or are tending to erode; whether the small group dominating the market has a constant or changing membership; whether a significant group of potential entrants is poised to move, should prices rise; and whether the producers with large market shares face powerful or dispersed buyers.

In short, while market power and market share are often closely related—the former deriving from the latter—they are not necessarily opposite sides of the same coin. A firm might produce a preponderant portion of some product but trigger a wave of new entrants by raising price. That firm has no market power. The same firm, were it able to wall out potential competition deliberately by frequent and indiscriminate patent infringement litigation, would have market power. The ability to earn very high profits that persist over many years may also be evidence of market power.

Some market power determinations examine whether customers of a particular branded product are a market by themselves and are thus subject to the market power of the product manufacturer. Are owners of Ford cars "locked in" to Ford-manufactured replacement parts, and does Ford therefore have market power in the replacement part market, even though Ford is confronted with brutal competition to sell its automobiles? The answer depends upon further examination of the factual record, but the point is that nothing may be assumed.

However determined, the existence of market power can be an extremely important clue in the search for competitive impact. In the absence of market power, certain business practices, no matter how objectionable on other legal grounds, cannot adversely affect competition and are therefore beyond the concern of the antitrust authorities.

SIX

Unilateral Activity

The antitrust laws apply to the actions of a single firm, acting alone, only in rare cases. Section 2 of the Sherman Act prohibits (1) attempted monopolization and (2) monopolization of a relevant market. Attempted monopolization is the use of improper tactics to *attain* monopoly status within a market; monopolization is the use of improper tactics to attain or *maintain* monopoly status or to extend it still further. Thus, the definition of *monopoly* is key.

Economists define *monopoly* as a market with a single seller. Antitrust law is less categorical. It defines a monopoly as a single firm that has market power, even though that firm has less than 100 percent of the market. *Market power* is defined as the power to control prices or exclude competition. Thus, in a correctly defined market, a firm that can raise price at will and with impunity, or has already done so, is a monopolist. That firm is a price maker, unlike a competitive firm, which is a price taker, unable to affect the level of prices by its own actions.

Using the market share shortcut for the definition of *market power*, the older cases taught that a single firm

36

with 75 to 80 percent or more of a relevant market would likely possess market power and therefore should be deemed a monopoly. Although the more recent cases make clear that market share alone is an inadequate basis upon which to conclude that a particular firm has attained monopoly status, the 75 to 80 percent guideline is, nevertheless, still a reliable shorthand indicator.

Remember that monopoly itself is only a threshold requirement for Section 2 application and is not itself illegal. That is so despite the fact that economists view monopoly power as an economic evil, whether lawfully or unlawfully acquired. To economists, monopoly means artificially high prices, restricted output, and stifled innovation.

Just because monopoly is bad in a theoretical economic sense, however, does not mean that it is illegal. And, in fact, there is nothing clearer in the antitrust laws than that pure, lawfully attained monopoly is not prohibited. That thought is sometimes expressed by courts when they say that monopoly power that results only from growth or development "as a consequence of a superior product, business acumen, or historic accident" is not objectionable (*United States v. Grinnell Corp.*, 384 U.S. 563 (1966)).

The practical point for business people, then, is that the antitrust laws do not prohibit tough, honest competition. That is, after all, the standard in the free enterprise system. Nor does that important rule change at all as the market share of a firm grows larger and larger: "The successful competitor, having been urged to compete, must not be turned upon when he wins" (*United States v. Aluminum Co. of America*, 148 F.2d 416 (2d Cir. 1945)). Although the antitrust laws have not always been clear and consistent on that point, at least today there is no doubt: large market shares alone are not illegal.

Where, then, lies the prohibited territory? The answer is, in two different directions: attempted monopolization and monopolization.

Attempt to Monopolize

If instead of tough, honest competition, the firm uses restraints of trade or unfair business tactics in an effort to attain monopoly status, that conduct is attempted monopolization and is illegal under Section 2. The conduct is illegal even if the firm has not yet attained actual monopoly status so long as a court can conclude that there is a "dangerous probability" that the plan to reach monopoly by smothering competition will be greeted with success. Most courts recognize that a dangerous probability can exist when a firm, acting improperly to attain monopoly status, achieves a market share of approximately 40 to 50 percent. Thus, a very large nationwide chain might be capable of attempting to monopolize; a neighborhood retail outlet employing the same business practices likely could not.

What the courts do require to prove an attempt to monopolize is some evidence of specific intent to destroy competition or build a monopoly. "Intent" in that context is not some psychological concept, to be wrung from the businessman in an unguarded moment on his psychiatrist's couch. It is, instead, determined by appraising each of his competitive tactics within the context of his overall behavior. Individual acts and practices, when viewed in isolation, may not appear indicative of anything, harmful or otherwise. But a pattern of actions, each one unexceptionable, may reflect an intent to monopolize. Just as one cannot form a judgment about a tapestry by studying only its individual threads, so one frequently cannot distinguish between competitive and anticompetitive behavior (per se offenses, such as price-fixing, aside) by looking at a specific act.

The requisite intent in that context, which goes well beyond the honest competitive urge to enlarge market share, can be revealed in two different ways. First, direct evidence of specific intent can be found, for instance, in the company's document files that house the chief executive officer's plan to do "whatever it takes to take over the market—and don't tell the lawyers." That document, when accompanied by some corroborative conduct that showed that the "plan" was more than a CEO's daydream or marketing hyperbole, would be direct evidence to support an allegation of attempted monopolization in violation of Section 2.

"While the completed offense of monopolization . . . demands only a general intent . . . a specific intent to destroy competition or build monopoly is essential to guilt for the mere attempt."
TIMES-PICAYUNE PUBLISHING CO. V. UNITED STATES, 345 U.S. 594, 626 (1953)

No such document need be found, however. Indirect evidence in the form of improper conduct will suffice. If a firm has engaged in a consistent pattern of predatory, exclusionary, or otherwise anticompetitive conduct that heads it in the direction of monopoly, that too can support a finding of an attempt to monopolize. A good way to think of the concept is that conduct may be improper if it is not rational from a business point of view but for its tendency to harm a competitor or undermine competition. Conduct that loses money in the short run because there is a hope that monopoly profits will be available in the long run is an example of that kind of predatory conduct.

Thus, for example, consistent pricing below cost with the predatory purpose of bankrupting the competition can support a claim of attempt to monopolize, when it is likely that the forgone profits will be recouped after the vanquished competitor has left the field. Bringing repetitive and baseless litigation against a faltering competitor is another example. A refusal to permit a competitor to use some facility that is essential for successful competition, without any business justification, has also been taken to support a finding of violation of Section 2. A railroad that owns the only bridge across a large river cannot arbitrarily deny its use, on reasonable terms, to a desperate competitor, if the denial will eventually drive that competitor out of business and leave the bridge owner the sole railroad in the market.

Monopolization

So much for the company that seeks monopoly status by improper means. What about the company that has attained monopoly status completely lawfully, merely by having a superior product or by being a more effective marketer? The road ahead for the lawful monopolist is a narrow one.

"Tolerated but not cherished" by the antitrust laws, the lawful monopolist may continue to do those things that are considered honestly competitive. It may continue to expand to meet demand, for instance; it may introduce innovative technology or an improved product; it may even charge as high a price for its product as the market will accept or as low a price as will cover its cost of production.

What the lawful monopolist may not do, however, is to attempt to suppress competition on the merits. It may not maintain or extend its market power by improper or unlawful conduct that is equivalent to a restraint of trade. Nor can it engage in unfair or unethical tactics. As with attempted monopolization, predatory or exclusionary behavior is ruled out.

"The offense of monopoly . . . has two elements: (1) the possession of monopoly power in the relevant market and (2) the willful acquisition or maintenance of that power as distinguished from growth or development as a consequence of a superior product, business acumen, or historic accident."

UNITED STATES V. GRINNELL CORP.,
384 U.S. 563, 570–571 (1966)

Some conduct is less clearly anticompetitive, however. In the case of truly ambiguous conduct, the key often is whether there is independent business justification. Refusal on the part of a monopolist to continue to cooperate in a joint marketing effort with a struggling rival, for instance, may be justified if the joint effort imposes undue costs on the monopolist. Such refusal may fall afoul of the law if it imposes no such costs but merely deprives the struggling competitor of access to important outlets—especially if accompanied by other unfair competitive tactics. If that refusal has the intended substantial adverse effects on the smaller rival and on consumers, it can be viewed as exclusionary. Ambiguity melts away, and the arbitrary refusal stands revealed as monopolization under Section 2.

A lawful monopolist may also step across the line if it uses its monopoly as leverage to increase its share in some other market. Thus, the local telephone company may violate Section 2 if it attempts to improve its position in the market for telephones by requiring that all telephones be purchased from it.

A monopolist is also on shaky ground if it undertakes, without justification based on efficiency, to raise barriers to entry by potential competitors, to raise the costs of rivals struggling to stay in the market, or to deprive them of fair access to customers. When the Aspen Skiing Company was found to have monopoly power, for example, it was faced with the necessity of providing a valid business justification for its refusal to continue a joint marketing program with its one, smaller competitor. It failed to provide a justification that satisfied the U.S. Supreme Court and paid substantial damages as a result.

In the past several years, Justice Department cases brought against Microsoft Corp. have explored familiar monopolization issues. One case challenged certain practices, not because they conferred a monopoly but because they contributed to the maintenance of it. Specifically, the Justice Department objected to a per-processor license that required payment of a royalty on all personal computers containing a particular processor, whether or not the machine contained a Microsoft operating system. The practical effect of the practice from the government's point of view was to impose a "tax" on the use of competing operating systems that made them less competitive. A consent decree agreed upon by Microsoft and the Justice Department banned that and other related conduct. Simultaneously, Microsoft and the European Commission reached a substantially identical settlement.

In a second case brought more recently, the allegations were that Microsoft had violated Section 2 in two different ways: first, it had monopolized the market for operating systems for Intel-compatible PCs by such tactics as maximizing the difficulties for applications written in competitive software, and second, it had attempted to monopolize the Internet browser market at least in part by trying to persuade Netscape not to offer competing browser software. Following trial, the lower court judge sustained both allegations and ordered the company broken into two separate companies. The appeals court affirmed the monopoly-maintenance charge but reversed the attempted monopolization finding because the government failed to carry its burden of showing a dangerous probability of reaching monopoly in a properly defined relevant market.

In summary, gaining monopoly by improper conduct violates Section 2. Maintaining or extending even a lawful monopoly by improper conduct also violates Section 2. Conduct in those circumstances is improper if it is other than competition on the merits.

SEVEN

Competitors

Relationships among competitors are subject to close scrutiny under the antitrust laws because they can so easily evolve into conspiracy that can destroy the competitive integrity of the marketplace. The most extreme forms of classic cartel behavior, such as price-fixing or division of markets, not only are per se unlawful but will trigger criminal prosecution.

"[A] combination formed for the purpose and with the effect of raising, depressing, fixing, pegging, or stabilizing the price of a commodity in interstate or foreign commerce is illegal per se."
UNITED STATES V. SOCONY-VACUUM OIL CO.,
310 U.S. 150, 223 (1940)

The fact of close scrutiny should not, however, drive business people to the opposite extreme. A broad range of permissible contact between competitors elicits little antitrust concern. Purely social contacts in which no business is discussed are obviously benign. Trade association memberships are unobjectionable if

44

the meetings are concerned with competitively neutral topics such as safety standards, or if prudent steps are taken to ensure that their activities do not taint a firm's sensitive competitive decisions. Industrywide lobbying for favorable legislation or regulation is permissible. Contacts that have legitimate purposes are safe. But contacts that are unexplained leave juries free to speculate, particularly if the contacts accompany otherwise suspicious, seemingly anticompetitive conduct.

Legally, the difference between permissible and impermissible contact among competitors depends upon whether an agreement exists. An agreement can be a written document or merely an oral exchange of assurances, or even hints, that competitors will pursue some coordinated plan. Furthermore, an agreement can be proven by using only circumstantial evidence. Direct evidence, such as a written document or the testimony of a renegade insider, is not necessary. As a result, agreements among competitors may be evidenced by such subtle practices as announcing revocable price increases before their effective date to invite competitors to join in future price changes, or offering customers low price guaranties to signal to rivals the intent not to cut prices. Although practices instituted to improve an individual company's competitiveness are safe from scrutiny, businesses should be particularly careful not to engage in any practice that can be justified economically only if a competitor follows suit.

Price-Fixing

Because pricing is so close to the heart of competition within the marketplace, agreements among competitors that fetter their pricing discretion pose an "actual or potential threat to the central nervous system of the economy" (*United States v. Socony-Vacuum Oil Co.,* 310 U.S. 150 (1940)).

"Naked" price-fixing presents the easiest case. Virtually all agreements among competitors that directly affect prices are held to be per se unlawful and can be the basis for criminal prosecution. A precise price need not be agreed upon. Prices are fixed within the meaning of the antitrust laws

> if the range within which purchases or sales will be made is agreed upon, if the prices paid or charged are to be at a certain level or on ascending or descending scales, if they are to be uniform, or if by various formulas they are related to market prices. They are fixed because they are agreed upon (*United States v. Socony-Vacuum Oil Co.,* 310 U.S. 222).

It is not a defense that the fixed price is reasonable or that it happens to be the same as the existing market price. It is likewise not a defense that only a portion of the price, such as a surcharge, is fixed; a conspiracy among competitors to fix or eliminate credit terms is also per se illegal price-fixing. The same harsh treatment is accorded agreements among competitors establishing uniform discounts, consistent pricing methods, or standard cash down-payment requirements. Thus, an automobile dealer association's circulation of a uniform price list, from which negotiations with the customer started but as a result of which no actual sale ever took place, was held unlawful. And it matters not whether the competitors are professionals, as for instance lawyers or doctors. Even a local bar association's minimum fee schedule, supervised by a state bar and the state supreme court, runs afoul of the law.

Finally, as with agreements to set minimum prices, maximum price-fixing agreements are unlawful. Against the argument that maximum price-fixing agreements may be justified by procompetitive effects, the Supreme Court said that price is simply too sensitive a subject to permit some price-fixing, even where procompetitive effects may arguably be expected. That prohibition against the collusive setting of price ceilings may, at first blush, seem contrary to the notion that competition serves consumers by keeping prices down. Not so. Price ceilings may discourage newcomers from entering an industry and reduce innovation and competition in the long run. The goal of antitrust policy is competitive prices, not high or low ones. Per se treatment and, as a result, criminal prosecutions remain the order of the day.

Bid-rigging is a form of direct price-fixing and is therefore flatly illegal, without any possibility of justification. Competitors that agree among themselves to rotate the winning bid, to bid uniformly low, or to bid in some other collectively determined, artificial manner are engaged in price-fixing.

Where the arrangement with competitors in pursuit of some valid objective is designed not to fix or stabilize prices directly, but nevertheless still has that incidental effect, the antitrust courts are willing to listen to the defense and to apply the rule of reason to the evidence they hear. Composers and performers would find it difficult individually to collect royalties due them from thousands of radio stations and other users of their music, so they are permitted to combine to issue a blanket license, covering all their music, even though in a literal sense the price charged for performance rights was affected. Such an arrangement

47

was necessary to create the blanket music license in the first place, with its efficient means of collecting royalties whenever and wherever the music is performed, and thus had a procompetitive justification.

"Not all arrangements among actual or potential competitors that have an impact on price are per se violations of the Sherman Act or even unreasonable restraints."
BROADCAST MUSIC, INC. V. COLUMBIA BROADCASTING SYSTEM, INC.,441 U.S. 1, 23 (1979)

The same analysis was applied, with a different result, to the National Collegiate Athletic Association and the restraints it imposed in connection with football broadcasting. To increase the value of its football broadcasts, the NCAA adopted a plan that limited the total amount of televised intercollegiate football, limited the number of games any one school could televise, and in separate exclusive agreements with two television networks set the price for particular telecasts. Evaluating the restraints under the rule of reason on the grounds that some horizontal restraints on competition were essential if the product was to be available at all, the Court nevertheless found those particular restraints excessive. The plan produced the fatal defects of higher price, lower output, and general unresponsiveness to consumer preference. Concluding that the NCAA could market its televised football just as effectively without the plan, the Supreme Court found the plan a violation of the Sherman Act.

In the absence of a justification, one professional association's rule against competitive bidding was held unlawful; so, too, was an agreement among automobile dealers to limit showroom hours.

On occasion, a seller will wish to check the truthfulness of a purchaser's assertion that the seller's competitor is offering a lower price. The temptation for the seller to ask the competitor directly, sometimes called price verification, should be resisted. The Supreme Court has made clear that discussions between competitors on price, even for apparently plausible purposes, are simply too fraught with danger to the competitive system to permit.

Many firms belong to trade associations whose very purpose may be to exchange industry information. The court decisions that focus on exchange of competitive information are quite consistent. In general, such exchanges are not prohibited, unless they have a direct effect on prices to be charged in future transactions. The best guideline is that the more current and specific the pricing information exchanged in the trade association forum, the more danger there is of antitrust illegality. The reason is obvious: the exchange of today's price lists—or worse still, tomorrow's—is more likely to engender follow-the-leader pricing than is the exchange of years-old data.

It bears repeating that, at the extreme end of the spectrum, where naked price-fixing is involved, criminal prosecution will invariably be the rule. Where, in contrast, price effects are the incidental consequences of attempts to achieve some valid purpose, although they may be unlawful as a civil matter, criminal prosecution is ruled out. The only exception, of course, is that situation where a supposedly lawful purpose is really only a sham to cloak a pure price-fixing agreement.

An interesting development is the FTC's attempt to use Section 5 of the Federal Trade Commission Act to reach invitations to collude on price in situations where apparently no actual agreement on price was ever concluded. The consent orders in three separate cases prohibit companies from inviting competitors to raise or fix prices by agreement.

Electronic commerce puts traditional price-fixing concerns in a fascinating new light. Price-fixing has traditionally involved meetings in "smoke-filled" rooms. The telephone then became a handy tool of conspirators. In the 1990s, the computerized airline reservation system was alleged to be a price-fixing device for airfares. Now, with so-called B2B markets popping up all over the Internet, sending pricing information across the globe and back virtually instantaneously, extra care will have to be taken to avoid the temptation to signal price movements in such a way as to give rise to an inference of agreement to fix prices, most often by sellers, but also by buyers.

Market Division

Market divisions are agreements among competitors to divide territory, customers, or product markets. An agreement between two competitors that one would do business only north of Main Street and the other only south would be a classic example. Such agreements are illegal per se under Section 1 of the Sherman Act. The displeasure of the Antitrust Division is likely to take the form of criminal prosecution.

It does not matter that the market divisions are not part of a price-fixing agreement, or that they split up a market in which neither does business or in which both do business. They are considered naked restraints of trade with no purpose except the stifling of competition. When two bar review courses agreed not to compete with each other in certain geographic areas, the Supreme Court held the arrangement per se unlawful.

Those arrangements are sharply distinguishable from covenants not to compete between a business and a former owner or employee of the business, who may nevertheless be a potential competitor. Such covenants incidental to the sale or dissolution of a business, or designed to help protect trade secrets or trade names, are evaluated under the rule of reason, because again they are incidental to a lawful and constructive purpose. Under the so-called ancillary restraints doctrine, which dates back to the 1899 Supreme Court decision in the *Addyston Pipe* case, if the restrictions are considered reasonable (that is, neither excessively long nor overly restrictive given the circumstances), they will be upheld. An agreement not to reenter the baking industry anywhere in the country, for example, might be held unreasonable, given the essentially local character of the business. But a similar nationwide restriction incident to the sale of, say, a professional services firm might be held to be reasonably related to the nature of the business being sold and therefore unobjectionable.

On occasion, an agreement among competitors to engage in a joint activity that involves some market allocation as a necessary part of an important and valuable objective of the enterprise will be evaluated by looking at the agreement's net contribution to competition. Joint production agreements may require the companies to produce complementary, but not overlapping, products. Although competition is to some extent lessened, the advantage of greater efficiency is sufficient justification.

Collective Refusals to Deal

Collective refusals to deal arise in a variety of competitive contexts. Sometimes they involve competitors, other times firms with vertical relationships. Sometimes they include a sufficient number of competitors to be able to deny the excluded firm access to suppliers or markets; sometimes that is not the case. And at times collective refusals to deal are demonstrably essential to the conduct of the business in which the parties are engaged.

Although no bright line can be drawn, it is possible to conclude that such agreements among competitors will come under closer scrutiny than will mere vertical arrangements, particularly if the parties possess market power. Thus, as with other practices, the boycott that seems always or almost always to restrict competition and decrease output is subject to per se treatment. Collective efforts by two competitors to deny to a third any access to absolutely necessary suppliers, for instance, will evoke per se treatment. Outright condemnation greeted competitors who banded together to procure the denial of necessary certification of a competitor's product, or who cut off important sources of news to a competitor newspaper, or who denied needed wholesale supplies of appliances to a competing retail outlet. The key in those cases seems to be that the boycott cuts off access to an essential supply or market, is frequently imposed by firms possessing a dominant position in the relevant market, and more often than not is not supported by plausible business and efficiency justifications. Those kinds of collective refusals to deal easily fall within the category of those agreements among competitors that are likely to produce anticompetitive effects and are therefore subject to per se condemnation.

But not every collective refusal to deal is so clearly anticompetitive. The Supreme Court has decided that a wholesale purchasing cooperative that excludes a potential competitor is not a form of concerted

---

"Unless the cooperative possesses market power or exclusive access to an element essential to effective competition, the conclusion that expulsion is virtually always likely to have an anticompetitive effect is not warranted."

NORTHWEST WHOLESALE STATIONERS, INC. V. PACIFIC STATIONERY & PRINTING CO., 472 U.S. 284 (1985)

---

activity that justifies per se treatment. Wholesale purchasing cooperatives must establish and enforce reasonable rules to function effectively, and the competitor can secure supplies from other sources.

In sum, as with other conduct, group boycotts that are naked horizontal restraints and have no purpose other than restricting output or raising prices are illegal per se. Other refusals to deal that are ancillary to a lawful main purpose, such as, for instance, the integration of economic functions of separate businesses by contract for certain efficiency purposes, must be judged under the rule of reason according to their purpose and effect. A law firm—in reality a collection of independent practitioners for efficiency purposes— or a sports league can refuse to deal, because each is on balance procompetitive. In the absence either of market power or of unique access to a business element necessary for effective competition, the collective refusal to deal is likely to be sustained.

Joint Ventures and Other Horizontal Agreements

Competitors agree with each other for a variety of reasons that have nothing to do with restriction of output or the fixing of prices. A variety of joint ventures between competitors, for instance, are designed to enable both to enter a market that neither could enter separately. Sometimes joint ventures are constructed to permit the pooling of complementary skills or the creation of economies of scale. The NCAA does for college athletics what no single college could do for itself. The same is true with Broadcast Music, Inc., and the American Society of Composers, Authors, and Publishers, the New York Stock Exchange, an electric power pool, or a nationwide bank credit card system. In each of those projects, the purposes are praiseworthy (respectively, efficient licensing of intellectual property; creation of a market in which to trade securities; movement of electricity to points of consumption; and nationwide availability of a service to consumers) and will normally withstand challenge under Section 1 of the Sherman Act. The key, in the words of the Federal Trade Commission, is that the necessary restraints are limited "to those inevitably arising out of dealings between partners, or necessary (and of no broader scope than necessary) to make the joint venture work" (*Brunswick Corp.*, 94 F.T.C. 1174, 1275 (1979)). That is a modern restatement of the ancient doctrine of ancillary restraints.

The focus on narrowly tailored ancillary restraints ensures that unnecessarily anticompetitive restrictions are deleted. The loss of that focus doomed those restrictions in the NCAA case that were found extraneous to the necessary functions of the association and therefore unduly anticompetitive. If the restrictions relate directly to price or output, the justifications must be very strong indeed.

In certain circumstances the antitrust laws encourage joint ventures between competitors to expand to include other competitors. Where participation in a joint venture is critical to competitive success, exclusion of any competitor from the venture's benefits may be challenged. If four of five mining companies in a mountain valley control the only means of access through a joint venture tunnel, denial of access on reasonable terms to the fifth may be found unlawful. But access will be compelled only when the excluded company is thereby unable to compete or if the purpose of the exclusion is anticompetitive, that is, not related to the purposes of the joint venture. In those situations the joint venture may be entitled to reasonable compensation for the risks it has already borne so that the prospective entrant does not become a "free rider." The issue of reasonableness in those circumstances is predictably murky and not easily decided.

In the 1980s, amid concern that the strict application of antitrust law to certain joint ventures was harming the international competitiveness of American companies, legislation was passed to confirm the applicability of the rule-of-reason standard to research or production joint ventures. In addition, those kinds of joint ventures, if they register in advance with the Justice Department and the FTC, are permitted, if found liable in a subsequent antitrust suit, to cap their liability at actual damages, rather than pay the usual treble damages.

More recently, to offer further comfort to would-be joint venturers, the Antitrust Division and the FTC issued guidelines on "competitor collaborations."

Described as not changing existing law, the new guidelines leave traditional per se analysis unchanged. If a transaction is not per se unlawful, the guidelines then establish an analytical framework of four economic inquiries having to do with competitive effect and offsetting efficiencies. Cutting across that elaborate analysis for any joint venture fortunate enough to qualify, two "safety zones" are established: a joint venture whose participants account for 20 percent or less of any relevant market affected by the joint venture is acceptable. Likewise, any research and development joint venture that faces three or more independent R&D competitors will escape censure.

EIGHT

Mergers and Acquisitions

The first antitrust law was passed in 1890 in response to a wave of mergers that led to the monopolization of several important industries. Mergers and acquisitions remain a subject of special interest today under the antitrust laws.

Section 7 of the Clayton Act is the controlling statute. First enacted in 1914, it was strengthened in 1950 and then again in 1980, so that it now prohibits any merger or acquisition "where in any line of commerce in any section of the country, the effect of such acquisition may be substantially to lessen competition, or to tend to create a monopoly."

The statute uses the words *may be* and is therefore sometimes called an incipiency statute. The statute has been construed to reach not only actual, realized anticompetitive effects, but also those that become probable, as a result of the merger. It makes no difference therefore whether the resulting firm has obtained actual market power or by aggregating significant market shares has merely set the stage.

It also makes no difference under the statute whether the merger is a stock acquisition, an assets acquisition, or a straight statutory merger. Nor does it make a difference whether the entities involved are technically corporations or operate as partnerships, joint ventures, or some other type of business entity. The statute applies—in different ways, of course—to all mergers between competitors (horizontal mergers), between customers and suppliers (vertical mergers), and between generally unrelated companies (conglomerate mergers).

Premerger Notification Procedures

Section 7A of the Clayton Act, more commonly called the Hart-Scott-Rodino Act, provides for the prior notification of most merger transactions to both the Federal Trade Commission and the Antitrust Division. No such merger may be consummated without complying with the notification procedures and awaiting the expiration of a statutorily defined waiting period.

In a typical case, parties to a merger attempt to file the requisite forms and basic merger documents with the agencies as soon as possible following the agreement to merge. After the two enforcement agencies decide—on the basis of industry experience and available resources—which of them will have responsibility for determining whether a potentially anticompetitive effect exists, the agency of choice will conduct a preliminary inquiry. Generally, if it is not already familiar with the industry involved—and it may well be—it will collect published information and conduct interviews, both with representatives of the parties and with competitors and customers within the industry. The agency may decide that there is no possibility of an anticompetitive effect and terminate the initial thirty-day waiting period early, thus permitting the parties to consummate the agreement immediately.

If, however, competitive questions remain, the agency will intensify its investigation and will compel the production of documents and oral testimony. Thirty days following the filing of the initial notification, the agency must decide whether it wishes to investigate further, or whether it is willing to allow the merger to take place. Assuming that important questions remain unresolved, and especially if the agency has already decided to sue to prevent the acquisition from taking place, the agency will send the parties an extensive demand for information, which is called a Second Request. Although the parties have an unlimited time in which to gather the information, because they are interested in getting to the end of the procedure so as to close the deal, that is frequently a period of frantic activity.

Once all requested information has been submitted to the enforcement agency, the agency then has twenty days to finish its investigation. At the end of that time, the parties may proceed to close. Frequently, if the agency needs further time, it will hope to persuade the parties to delay the consummation. If the agency cannot do so, it must be prepared to file suit in federal court to prevent the merger from taking place.

An important part of that process, as with investigations of other possible violations, is the opportunity for meetings with personnel from the enforcement agencies. Frequently, those meetings involve lawyers and their clients as well as expert economists and will be detailed, searching, and intensive. Those meetings can be crucial. In most years premerger notification filings are required for approximately 2,000 mergers—

although in recent merger-wave years, the number more than doubled—but suits are eventually filed in only 4 percent—and frequently the quality of advocacy throughout the entire process, and especially at those meetings, makes the critical difference. As we noted earlier, preparation for those meetings should be as painstaking as preparation for a trial.

An issue sometimes addressed at those meetings is whether the agency's concerns can be resolved by altering the transaction to eliminate anticompetitive features. The parties' officers are consulted immediately, and a short but intensive negotiation takes place. If the deadline for filing the lawsuit is imminent, the agency will demand that it be extended for the short period of time required to complete the negotiation or to conclude that the effort is futile. Obviously, the price of declining to consent to the extension is an immediate lawsuit.

If, notwithstanding those efforts, suit is filed, a shortened hearing will likely be held in court on the narrow issue of whether to halt the acquisition temporarily, pending the opportunity for full trial. Frequently, an order will be issued postponing consummation, and a full trial on the merits will be scheduled for several months later. That delay has the inevitable effect of cooling the ardor of one or both companies for the corporate marriage. It is not at all uncommon, even at that late stage, for the parties to attempt once again to resolve the enforcement agency's competitive concerns by agreeing to reformat the transaction or to spin off various assets to moot the competitive concerns of the enforcement agency.

In the absence of settlement, trial on the merits may go forward, with the resultant delay; alternatively, the parties, tired of the hassle and faced with the impatience of the financial markets, may abandon the transaction.

A further layer of complexity and frustration for the parties results from the fact that state attorneys general and private parties may also bring enforcement actions. We address some of the technicalities of those kinds of claims below. Suffice it to say for now that state attorneys general have filed numerous challenges to mergers, particularly where the anticompetitive effects are thought to be particularly harsh within a specific state. Private parties also challenge mergers on a regular basis, but courts may prevent their claims from proceeding to trial where those parties are in essence claiming injury merely from the procompetitive efficiencies resulting from the merger, which the antitrust laws purport to encourage and not to prohibit. Notwithstanding all those limitations, merging parties ignore such threats at their peril.

Horizontal Mergers

A horizontal merger—an acquisition by one competitor of another—is of immediate interest to the antitrust agencies. A horizontal merger eliminates competition between competitors far more surely than does any agreement in restraint of trade—and the elimination of competition may be permanent. Three anticompetitive effects are highlighted: first, the surviving firm may have assembled the instruments of dominance; second, the market, with uncertainty reduced, is more susceptible to collusion; and third, the merged firm may itself be able to raise prices unilaterally. But at the same time, horizontal mergers may also advance the potential for procompetitive effects, including the achievement of otherwise unattainable efficiencies.

There are two stages at which the merits of the merger are considered—the first by the enforcement agencies and the second by the courts. Unsurprisingly, the standards of the two are not the same. During the premerger notification phase, when the enforcement agency is investigating to determine whether to bring suit, it applies its own standards. While they are not entirely unrelated to the relevant case law, which will be applied later if suit is ever brought, they are set out from time to time as written guidelines, which do not in themselves have any binding legal effect but which will in fact usually determine the result within the agency.

Merger guidelines were first issued in 1968 by the Antitrust Division and then revised in 1982 and 1984, and again in 1992 and 1997. While the guidelines do not in any sense supersede the law, they do attempt to indicate when the Antitrust Division—and now also the FTC—are likely to challenge a merger.

The guidelines proceed in a way that will now be familiar to our readers. First, they require that the relevant market be defined (as described in chapter 5). Once defined, the market is placed in one of three categories: unconcentrated, moderately concentrated, or highly concentrated. Those market segments are given precise numerical boundaries by reference to the market shares of all competitors in the marketplace. Sometimes the guidelines speak in terms of plain percentages; most often they refer to the Herfindahl-Hirschman index, which involves the arithmetic manipulation of market share percentages to produce a result less obscure than it at first sounds. For those curious to learn how those computations are done, we suggest appendix B.

As an initial matter, the guidelines state that in an unconcentrated market, no merger of any size will be prosecuted. In a moderately concentrated market, only large mergers that lead to greater market concentration will trigger antitrust concern. Finally, in a highly concentrated market, almost any merger will excite the enforcement agency's prosecutorial attention.

After that quantitative analysis is completed, the guidelines direct the agency to look at a variety of other market factors, in addition to market concentration, that bear on competitive effects. The premise is that merger policy today focuses primarily on preventing mergers that would allow firms to engage in "coordinated interaction" that results in harm to consumers. The term *coordinated interaction* covers all kinds of conduct by which firms seek to profit by working together as a group rather than by each one's pursuing its own individual self-interest. Such behavior could include price-fixing, which is illegal in and of itself; or tacit collusion, which is more ambiguous; or even classic oligopoly behavior, which is likely not illegal. So the agency will attempt to determine whether postmerger market conditions would be conducive to reaching terms of coordination and detecting and punishing deviations from those terms.

A record of previous express collusion by firms in the relevant market would certainly be a telling clue. Likewise, a market in which the products were very similar, pricing was standardized, and competitive information was widely available would be subjected to very close scrutiny. Weighing against the merger would be the facts that specific transactional information is freely available and that transactions are frequent. Weighing in favor of a merger would be the existence in the market of maverick and disruptive firms that refuse to adhere to market pricing patterns.

Even in the absence of indications that a merger will lead to coordinated interaction, the agency may still be concerned that the merged firm may itself be able to raise prices unilaterally. For example, in a market characterized by product differentiation, a merger that combines the first and second choices of many consumers may well lead to price rises to certain classes of customers, regardless of whether all competitors join the increase.

The guidelines next point the agency's investigation to the possibility that a potential competitor might enter the market and relieve any anticompetitive pressure the merger creates—such as less vigorous price competition. If entry would be easy, inexpensive, and relatively immediate, and therefore likely, the enforcement agency is unlikely to sue. Very high capital expenditures and a long lead time required for entry point to the existence of high entry barriers, which make suit more likely. Under the guidelines, entry is thought to be timely if it would likely occur within two years.

The 1997 revision to the guidelines allows recognition of efficiencies in the competitive effects analysis. The efficiencies must be unique to the particular transaction, so that they cannot reasonably be accomplished by means short of merger. But if it is plausible that the merger will help the parties attain efficiencies not otherwise available to them and that those efficiencies would be sufficient to reverse the merger's potential harm to consumers, then the enforcement agencies may well not challenge the acquisition. What seems to be contemplated is a sliding scale: only extraordinarily great efficiencies will be sufficient to prevent challenge to a merger that would otherwise involve extensive potential adverse competitive effects.

Finally, there is the so-called failing-firm defense. A merger will not be challenged, in all probability, if the acquired firm is unlikely to be able to meet its financial obligations in the future, would not likely survive a bankruptcy reorganization, and has made a good-faith—though unsuccessful—effort to find an alternative and less anticompetitive purchaser. The most recent version of the guidelines added the requirement that, absent the acquisition, the assets of the failing firm would exit the relevant market.

If the agency decides to sue in federal court, the guidelines become legally irrelevant, and the judge will instead apply case law. That body of law has been built up over the years since the enactment of Section 7 of the Clayton Act, although the development has involved several major and fundamental changes in direction and emphasis. Even so, the case law has the same competitive concerns as do the guidelines and shares the same general approach: first define the market and then analyze the competitive significance of the proposed merger. Nevertheless, the emphasis in several places is significantly different and potentially friendlier to the parties defending the acquisition.

Under the current case law, market shares at the time of the merger are only the beginning point. They are used to establish a presumption of illegality. The precise level at which that presumption is triggered, however, has changed remarkably over the years. As recently as the late 1960s, aggregate market shares of under 10 percent in a relatively unconcentrated Los

Angeles grocery store market were sufficient to support a finding of unlawfulness. Since that time, the triggering point for illegality has risen steadily. In the 1970s, acquisitions that resulted in aggregate shares of approximately 10 to 20 percent could be held unlawful. More recently, the courts may well approve aggregate concentration in excess of 25 percent.

"[O]nly a further examination of the particular market— its structure, history and probable future—can provide the appropriate setting for judging the probable anticompetitive effect of the merger."

BROWN SHOE CO. V. UNITED STATES,
370 U.S. 294, 322 n.38 (1962)

Without an easy bright-line rule, the courts and the Federal Trade Commission examine factors beyond market share to see whether the presumptive illegality can be rebutted by the showing of the absence of any anticompetitive effect. Sometimes mere market share statistics fail to tell the whole story: they may be a measurement of the wrong index of competitive capability, or they may not sufficiently account for dynamic changes in the marketplace. The fact that reserves are either depleted or already committed by long-term contracts with large customers would possibly not show up in the market share data based on capacity, but they would be crucial to the merger's true competitive significance. For even if the merging firms control a small share of total capacity, their hold on a large share of uncommitted capacity may give the new entity substantial market power. Likewise, foreign sales of a multinational corporation may or may not be significant, depending on tariff or import restrictions.

Increasingly, even where market shares seem high by historical standards, each of these factors will weigh in the judge's mind against a finding of unlawfulness: low barriers to new entry, the existence on the other side of the market of large business entities that will prevent the merged companies from exercising market power, a lack of evidence that collusion is likely, or the existence of potential competitors ready to enter the market if the merged company raises prices sharply.

The net result seems to be this: the larger the market shares controlled by the merging parties, the more likely it is that a court will find illegality. That is particularly true at the preliminary injunction stage, before a full trial on the merits during which other factors can be examined with greater care. The more concentrated the industry generally, the lower that triggering point for illegality will be. But even in a concentrated market in which the merging companies have relatively high aggregate market shares, most courts are willing to look beyond the numbers to discern the competitive reality. The opportunity thus exists to persuade fact finders that the government's numbers tell an incomplete story, that factors exist in the marketplace to attenuate the market power of any proposed combination, and that at the end of the day the merger of competitors will not produce an inefficient and anticompetitive result.

Vertical Mergers

Vertical mergers—mergers between suppliers and customers—have received scant attention from the enforcement agencies over the years, but somewhat more in recent years. The guidelines certainly recognize that in theory vertical mergers could be unlawful to the extent that they create or increase barriers to entry, facilitate collusion, or, where regulated industries are involved, create the likelihood of evasion of rate regulation. On the other hand, vertical mergers frequently result in more efficient performance—by reducing transaction costs, improving coordination of design or distribution, and lowering prices. Balancing anticompetitive effects against efficiencies is particularly difficult, and therefore controversial, with vertical mergers.

Nevertheless, the enforcement agencies have begun to mount cases against certain vertical mergers in recent years. In general, the cases are premised on the danger of vertical acquisitions in networked industries—cable, telecommunications, computers—where a firm with market power can discriminate against or foreclose access to a competitor in an upstream or downstream market. None of the recent cases has resulted in a judicial decision; each has been resolved by an agreed-upon consent decree narrowly tailored to address the enforcement agency's concern.

In the few cases brought by private parties within the industry, without the benefit of government intervention, the vertical merger has generally not been found anticompetitive. Although there are theoretical bases in the earlier cases for finding certain kinds of vertical mergers unlawful—for instance, where they involve markets with very few firms, or where disruptive buyers or sellers are eliminated—almost all vertical mergers are likely to escape challenge under the antitrust laws.

Conglomerate Mergers

Mergers between unrelated firms (mergers that are neither horizontal nor vertical) are termed conglomerate mergers. They range across a spectrum from pure conglomerate mergers (in which there is absolutely no relationship between the parties) to mergers in which one firm acquires another selling either related or complementary products or selling the same products in different geographic areas.

Through their guidelines, the government agencies have announced that they will file suit against conglomerate mergers only where there is a substantial risk of the elimination of important potential competitors—the first cousin of the horizontal merger problem, except that the "competition" that is eliminated is still potential. Describing such acquisitions as "not invariably innocuous," the guidelines focus on the elimination of a competitive threat at the edge of the market that affects the behavior of firms already in the market, or, alternatively, the elimination of the possibility of entry by a firm in a more procompetitive manner than by merger. The potential competition concerns will trigger enforcement action only when the market is very highly concentrated, entry barriers exist, the potential competitor eliminated has a substantial advantage in entering the market over other potential entrants, and the market share of the firm already within the market is well above 5 percent. Challenge is very likely if the market share is 20 percent or more. Suppose that a highly concentrated market of three sellers would raise prices in lock step but for the existence of a powerful firm outside—but on the edge of—the market and poised to enter if a profitable opportunity presents itself. The enforcement guidelines would disapprove of an acquisition by one of the three incumbent firms of the potential entrant. But in recent years, despite those pronouncements, very few cases have been brought, virtually none successfully, either by government or by private parties.

Very occasionally, conglomerate mergers are held unlawful on other grounds, particularly in the lower courts. Several cases have disapproved a merger in which the dominant market power of one party was thought to be "entrenched," or strengthened beyond easy challenge, by virtue of its access to the financial or other resources of the other merging party. But with those very few exceptions, conglomerate mergers are no longer of much interest to the antitrust authorities.

NINE

Relations with Customers

We have looked at relationships among competitors in all their manifold variety, from conspiracy in restraint of trade to joint venture to merger. Now, we examine agreements between businesses at different levels of the market. The Sherman Act's prohibition of contracts, combinations, and conspiracies in restraint of trade applies not only to relations among competitors (discussed in chapter 7), but also to restrictions contained in agreements with customers. Those restrictions govern the sale or distribution of the manufacturer's goods.

It is of course a fact that a manufacturer can always invest its own capital and use its own employees to form a distribution system, a step that would give it complete control. So even a very restrictive agreement with independent distributors leaves that sector freer of manufacturer control than it would be were the manufacturer to integrate vertically. The relevant economic question, then, is whether the vertical restriction is more anticompetitive than the manufacturer's establishment of its own distribution system.

Those economic facts have greatly influenced the legal treatment of vertical restraints over the years. Some practices, such as vertical nonprice restraints, for example, requiring a dealer to sell only to customers in New Jersey or only to certain classes of customers, have been categorized in the past as per se unlawful under Section 1 but are now evaluated under the rule of reason. The change of attitude was triggered by the realization that vertical restrictions have procompetitive effects as well as anticompetitive effects and that in some cases the former outweigh the latter. If by rigorous control of dealers, the manufacturer of a certain brand of product can improve its product's performance against its competitors', the antitrust courts now permit such restraints, notwithstanding a dampening of competition between one of the manufacturer's dealers and another. Strengthening interbrand competition is thought to be of more significance than the apparent weakening of intrabrand competition.

Having laid out the economic analysis, however, we remind our readers that economics influences antitrust law but does not determine it. That caution is especially pertinent when we consider vertical price-fixing.

Vertical Price Restraints

Manufacturers may sometimes wish to set the prices at which their distributors sell to retail customers. The interests of manufacturers and their distributors and retailers may at times diverge. The distributor might be satisfied with low volumes and high margins that deprive the manufacturer of economies of scale that might be available in the production process. Or he might find it in his interest to use a manufacturer's high-prestige item as a traffic-generating loss leader, thereby undermining the manufacturer's entire sales and advertising program. In the first instance, the manufacturer would want to set a maximum price; in the second, a minimum.

The urge to set a minimum price is more frequent. Most often, manufacturers set minimum resale prices to preserve the product's appeal as an upscale product or to prevent a "free-rider" problem in which discount stores siphon business away from full-service dealers who provide point-of-sale demonstrations but lose the sale. It is also argued that minimum price restrictions ensure that dealers will have the resources to provide desired customer services, such as repairs.

Under Section 1 of the Sherman Act, however, the setting of minimum resale prices is per se unlawful. Indeed, minimum resale price maintenance was first held unlawful in 1911. But although the Supreme Court has formally declined to vary its frequently criticized rule on the per se treatment of vertical minimum price restrictions, it has narrowed the effect of the rule by adjusting the legal concept of vertical agreement.

Consider the following possibilities. Suppose that a manufacturer announces that he wishes his price to the ultimate consumer to be X and that he will exercise his own independent discretion as to parties with whom he will deal. The message is loud and clear that there is a strong possibility that a dealer who fails to sell the product at the price of X will be terminated. Some view that kind of announcement as vertical price-fixing without an explicit agreement. Not so the courts.

That small chink in the per se rule was the beginning of a trend. The Supreme Court later widened the chink when it held that a dealer that did not comply with the suggested prices and was terminated after the manufacturer received complaints from other dealers did not necessarily have a valid antitrust complaint because, on those facts alone, there was no agreement of the kind required to trigger the Sherman Act. Then, in another expansion, the Court concluded that vertical price-fixing requires some agreement, explicit or implicit, on "price or price levels" (*Business Electronics Corp. v. Sharp Electronics Corp.*, 485 U.S. 717 (1988)).

"There must be evidence that tends to exclude the possibility that the manufacturer and nonterminated distributors were acting independently."
MONSANTO CO. V. SPRAY-RITE SERVICE CORP.,
465 U.S. 752, 764 (1984)

All those cases have reduced the applicability of the Sherman Act by limiting the concept of agreement, but none of them has overruled the per se rule against resale price maintenance. The result seems to be that an outright and explicit vertical agreement to fix minimum prices will produce per se treatment, but that less direct efforts by a manufacturer to influence retail prices will not.

As to maximum resale price maintenance, the Supreme Court has recently changed the rules. Overruling thirty years of precedent, the Court found that per se treatment was inappropriate for a type of conduct that could, on occasion, benefit both consumers and competition. Instead, vertical maximum price-fixing should now be evaluated under the rule of reason to identify those specific situations in which such price maintenance amounts to anticompetitive conduct (*State Oil Co. v. Khan*, 118 S. Ct. 275 (1997)).

What can the manufacturer do as a practical matter to attempt to influence the price at which his product is ultimately sold to the consumer, beyond the announcement and termination routinely sanctioned by the courts? He may, of course, suggest prices to the dealers, and they may wish to charge the specified price without any resistance. Manufacturers can certainly assist the dealers in reaching that result by providing price lists or promotional materials that specify the desired price. Danger arises when the manufacturer exceeds those "persuasive" tactics and uses coercive measures that interfere with the dealers' freedom to exercise their pricing discretion independently. Sanctions for deviation from suggested prices, policing, retaliatory wholesale price increases, and short-term leases that appear to be aimed at coercing dealers all support a finding of unlawful vertical price-fixing.

Courts have consistently held that promotional allowances and dealer-assisted programs are valid as long as dealers remain free to set their own price. Even rebates provided directly to the customers have been upheld for the same reason. Nevertheless, if any of those are reduced or withdrawn because of the dealer's failure to adhere to the manufacturer's suggested retail price, they would then appear to be an unlawful effort to coerce the dealer.

As a practical matter, federal enforcement authorities only occasionally bring cases in that area. Far more common are cases brought by private parties, including particularly dealers that are terminated, allegedly on grounds of failure to adhere to suggested prices. State attorneys general may also find such cases attractive.

Vertical Nonprice Restraints

Vertical nonprice restraints are limitations the manufacturer imposes on a distributor or retailer in any one of several forms that do not directly affect price. They may be location clauses, regulating the place from which a dealer may sell. They may be territorial or customer restrictions, regulating the area or the customers that the firm may serve. They may be exclusive distributorships, assigning one area exclusively to one firm. They may also be primary responsibility clauses, which assign specific areas to dealers with a required level of sales and service. Vertical nonprice restraints are frequently accompanied by profit pass-over clauses, requiring firms making sales in another dealer's territory to remit part of the profit to the host dealer.

That type of conduct, as distinguished from vertical price restraints, is not per se unlawful and is judged under the rule of reason. Vertical restrictions frequently reduce intrabrand competition because they tend to limit the number of sellers competing for the business of a given group of buyers. Such effects, however, may well be outweighed by the tendency of those restraints to promote interbrand competition. They frequently allow the

---

"Interbrand competition is the competition among the manufacturers of the same generic product . . . and is the primary concern of antitrust law."

CONTINENTAL TV, INC. V. GTE SYLVANIA, INC.,
433 U.S. 36, 52 n.19 (1977)

---

manufacturer to attain efficiencies in the distribution of his products, for example, by inducing aggressive retailers to make the optimal level of investment in the product's distribution. The Supreme Court has held that interbrand competition is the primary concern of the antitrust law, so that even if a vertical nonprice restraint produces effects on interbrand competition and intrabrand competition that are evenly balanced, the restraint will be sustained because interbrand competition is the more important.

The result seems to be, therefore, that most vertical nonprice restraints will be upheld against antitrust challenge. The sole exceptions would be in those rare circumstances where there is no interbrand competition to be weighed against the diminution of intrabrand competition.

Once again, those cases are overwhelmingly likely to be brought by private parties who believe themselves abused by the imposition of such restraints, and in recent years they have rarely been successful.

Tying Arrangements

A tying arrangement is defined as the conditioning of the sale of one product on the buyer's purchase of another product. The first is referred to as the tying product, the second as the tied product. The sale of desired hospital services only to a patient who also purchased anesthesiology services has been held to be a tying arrangement.

A tying arrangement may be challenged under Section 1 of the Sherman Act as an agreement in restraint of trade, under Section 3 of the Clayton Act, or under Section 5 of the Federal Trade Commission Act. The standards are the same in all cases.

The most common form of tying arrangement assumes that a seller has market power with respect to the tying product and can use that market power to leverage increased sales in the market for the tied product. Tying may also be expected where the sale of both products together produces economies of scale. Economies of scale, for instance, may permit a publisher to charge an advertiser little more for advertising in both a morning and an evening newspaper than in either one alone. Even though the advertiser is free to advertise solely in either paper, the rate inducement to buy both is sufficient to make that a tying arrangement, and a competing morning newspaper will likely complain.

"[T]he essential characteristic of an invalid tying arrangement lies in the seller's exploitation of its control over the tying product to force the buyer into the purchase of a tied product."

JEFFERSON PARISH HOSPITAL DISTRICT NO. 2
v. HYDE, 466 U.S. 2, 12 (1984)

It is said that tying arrangements are unlawful per se under the Sherman Act. As with boycotts, this is an instance where the per se rule can be applied only after some inquiry into market circumstances.

The elements of the inquiry include the following: two separate products must be involved; the sale of one must be conditioned on the purchase of another; the seller must have sufficient market power with respect to the tying product to enforce the tie; and the tying arrangements must not be purely theoretical or completely trivial in their impact on commerce. If all those elements can be shown, then the tying arrangement is presumed to be anticompetitive per se, without elaborate demonstration of adverse effect on competition. But note that each of those elements requires some factual exploration. And even if the tying arrangement is not found subject to per se treatment, it still may be invalidated under the rule of reason.

The two-product requirement is usually easily solved. Some products cannot usefully be sold separately. There is no separate market for left shoes without the right. Whether that "tying" arrangement is objectionable or whether the pair of shoes is in fact one product is the kind of question antitrust courts are called upon to answer. In general, whether there are two products is determined, not on the basis of the functional relationship between the two products, but on the character of demand for them. If the buying public perceives two separate and completely distinguishable products, then the courts are likely to find that two products exist. Right and left shoes are parts of one product: a pair of shoes. Copying machines and the paper they use are not.

The presence of a tie is likewise not usually difficult to analyze. In the absence of an explicit agreement requiring the purchase as a condition of the sale, courts will accept proof suggesting any kind of coercion by the seller or unwillingness to take the second product by the buyer. Similarly, the requirement that there be sufficient economic power with respect to the tying product seems redundant, at least where the complaint is brought by a customer claiming to have been coerced. The requisite market power, says the Supreme Court, is whatever is required to "force a purchaser to do something he would not do in a competitive market." How else could the tying arrangement be successfully imposed? There is a tendency to conclude that if the tie exists and is at all successful, then the requisite economic power is thereby demonstrated. The final requirement that there be a substantial amount of commerce affected by the restraint means only that the tie has more than a trivial impact in the market for the tied product.

A limited number of defenses against allegations of unlawful tying exist. The first is that the two components actually can be purchased separately: a new automobile can be obtained without having to purchase a stereophonic sound system—in short, no forced tying. Real tying arrangements are rarely successfully defended. Some few are sustained where, during the development period of a new industry, it was important to ensure effective functioning of complicated equipment by selling one integrated system. Or if tying arrangements are the only available way to avoid confusion or deception, or to avoid unwanted disclosure of trade secrets, they are also occasionally found lawful.

In a recent high-profile appellate decision, the court analyzed Microsoft's practice of integrating additional software functionality into its operating system and concluded that per se treatment was inappropriate: the evaluation of the legality of tying arrangements involving platform software products raised novel issues better handled under a rule-of-reason analysis. Although not concluding that per se treatment was improper for software markets generally, the court was worried that rigid application of per se rules to that new kind of integration would preclude a sensitive balancing of the conduct's anticompetitive harms in the tied product market against any procompetitive justifications.

Exclusive Dealing

Exclusive dealing is a requirement that a buyer buy only from a particular seller or vice versa. Commonly, such arrangements are termed requirements contracts or output contracts. They may be challenged under Section 1 of the Sherman Act, Section 3 of the Clayton Act, and Section 5 of the Federal Trade Commission Act.

The effect of exclusive dealing arrangements falls on competitors of the supplier, who are foreclosed for the period of time involved from marketing their products to a particular buyer, or on the buyer who is denied access to the committed supplier. Because they may have procompetitive effects, exclusive dealing arrangements are subject to rule-of-reason treatment. Thus, in addition to the amount of foreclosure (expressed as a market share percentage) and the length of the term of the arrangement, analysis of an exclusive dealing arrangement will examine any procompetitive justifications, such as the need of a new manufacturer to have dealers devoted to his product. The analysis will also consider business justifications such as the need of an electric utility for a reliable supply of consistently priced coal of the same quality. Other factors that may be considered in the analysis include the extent to which new entrants can easily find alternative distributors or suppliers, the trend in market shares of manufacturers of the relevant products, and the vigor of interbrand competition.

Price Discrimination

Manufacturers often wonder whether they can charge different prices for the same product to competing buyers. The question is answered in the negative by Section 2 of the Clayton Act, as amended by the Robinson-Patman Act. That act by and large makes it unlawful to discriminate in price between different buyers in certain circumstances. But because the statute is so highly technical, guidelines are difficult.

The prices to be compared must be charged to different buyers who made purchases at roughly the same time. In addition, the prices must be the actual net prices after all discounts, rebates, and the like. Moreover, the statute applies to commodities, not to the sale of services.

Finally, the price discrimination must cause competitive injury. Injury may occur at the level of the seller's competitor, at the level of the customers, or at the level of a customer of the disfavored customer, who finds himself competing at a disadvantage with customers of the favored customer.

A price alleged to be discriminatory may be justified where it is designed "in good faith to meet an equally low price of a competitor." Where a manufacturer seeks to rely on such a defense, it is well to keep in the files a record of the evidence of an equally low price of a competitor upon which the manufacturer relied. Likewise, there is a narrow defense based on detailed cost justification. Where it costs less to serve a particular customer, either because of volume, a slower delivery schedule, or other sound reasons, the ultimate price to that customer may recognize that cost difference. Here, too, it is important to make a record of those cost differences in case the lower prices are later challenged as discriminatory.

Finally, there is a third statutory defense where changing conditions in the market, such as distress sales, sales in dissolution of a business, or sales forced by a deterioration of perishable goods, make a lower price reasonable.

A companion to the price discrimination provision of the Robinson-Patman Act is the brokerage provision found in Section 2(c) of the Clayton Act. That provision, designed to prevent a price discrimination disguised as a fictitious brokerage fee, prohibits the grant of a commission or brokerage fee except for services rendered. Commercial bribery may also be a violation of Section 2(c).

Other provisions of the Robinson-Patman Act prohibit giving advertising or promotional allowances or services to customers if they are not freely available to competing customers on proportionally equal terms. Again, the statute is technical, but an advertising program that appears not to favor one set of customers or to disfavor another and is truly available across the board to all customers is not likely to violate the statute.

Finally, it is a violation to induce or knowingly receive a discriminatory price. That provision is designed to prohibit pure power buying.

The federal government now rarely enforces the Robinson-Patman Act: the enforcement authorities view it as an anachronistic remainder from depression-day efforts to spare mom-and-pop grocers the rigors of competition from emerging chain stores. To the enforcement authorities, the act seems to protect competitors rather than competition.

Private plaintiffs rely more heavily on the Robinson-Patman Act. But its highly technical provisions make such lawsuits difficult, and trial court awards are frequently reversed at the appeals stage.

Vertical Refusals to Deal

When a manufacturer refuses to establish or continue a relationship with a distributor, that refusal can be and often is challenged as a violation of the Sherman Act. Vertical refusals to deal that have the effect of enforcing resale price maintenance agreements or other restraints of trade run afoul of the Sherman Act.

Refusals to deal are often occasioned by efficiency concerns or business justifications and are therefore examined under the rule of reason. Unsatisfactory performance, financial difficulty, and failure to meet quality standards are all sufficient business justifications to support a refusal to deal. Vertical refusals to deal will also be sustained if it can be shown that they have no adverse effect on competition because alternative sources of supply are available or that one distributor can easily be substituted for another.

Government enforcement authorities do not file those cases or at least have not done so in recent decades. But private parties do: dealers, upset at being terminated by suppliers, frequently attack such vertical refusals to deal and win damage awards where the circumstances surrounding their termination strike juries as anticompetitive.

TEN

Intellectual Property

In a world in which intellectual capital is rapidly replacing physical capital as the cornerstone of the wealth of nations, nothing could be more important than sensitively applying the antitrust laws to intellectual property rights. That is no easy chore. Intellectual property is developed by both corporate research departments and the fabled lone inventor working in his garage in response to the prospects of substantial rewards. The risks that a research effort will come to naught, that some other inventor will beat the putative innovator to the finish line, and that an invention or innovation will seem feasible in the laboratory but prove too costly or perhaps even impossible to produce in marketable quantities all point to the need to protect intellectual property so that the rewards of success are sufficient to attract the needed financial and intellectual capital to the game.

The level of those rewards is directly related to the innovator's ability to deprive others of the use of his invention or trade secret. Making the intellectual property available to all who would use it hastens its introduction or broadens its use, but at the same time doing so seriously reduces the incentive to create such property in the first place. The antitrust laws must accommodate the tension between the desire to encourage invention, innovation, and the ongoing march of technology and productivity, and the desire to optimize the rate of diffusion of new discoveries.

The first of those goals—maximizing the pace of innovation—calls for the protection of intellectual property rights. To the extent that an innovator cannot appropriate to himself the benefits of his work, his incentive to struggle on is diminished. When so-called free riders can use the results without sharing in the costs of research and development, the private sector will invest less in research than is in the nation's interest. So we have laws granting innovators the right to the fruits of their labors, laws that provide for the patenting of inventions and the perpetual protection of trade secrets.

But that first goal also requires care. Intellectual property protection must not be improvidently granted or excessive in scope, lest subsequent innovators be discouraged in their task by the prospect that their own reward might be appropriated by an owner of intellectual property rights undeservedly overbroad in scope.

The second goal—rapid diffusion of new inventions and techniques—is met in several ways. The law permits the inventor to gain the benefits of economies of scale by licensing his invention to others, thereby spreading the fixed costs of research and development over the output of those licensees. It at the same time protects his stake in his invention by permitting him to restrict licensees' use of his work in any way that maximizes its value. Absent such a guarantee, the inventor's incentive to license his work to others would be diluted. And in the case of patents, the law requires the inventor to make his invention public to spur innovative activity on the part of others.

Equally important, rapid diffusion of innovation is ensured by preserving a competitive marketplace. The developer of a new product or process may wish to control the pace at which that innovation is introduced and to maintain the price of the product or process at a level that yields monopoly profits. But he must always reckon with the possibility that some equally talented innovator or equally well-funded research laboratory will come up with a superior product or a more efficient method of production. And the antitrust laws will ensure that channels of distribution are not unfairly denied and that those with a stake in the status quo cannot conspire to make it difficult for the new product to obtain such manufacturing and financial support as it may be able to command.

The tension seen in the competing economic policies is therefore reflected in the federal law that governs the world of intellectual property. Simple lawfulness under the patent laws does not necessarily dispose of the issue under the antitrust laws. The policies behind the two sets of federal law are not identical.

Nor are they truly in conflict. Instead, they represent complementary systems, designed in the long run to achieve maximum consumer welfare through the encouragement of both innovation, which is one of the chief engines of competition, and competition understood more broadly.

The development of the antitrust laws' application to intellectual property has been marred by a failure to understand that uneasy complementarity. Traditionally, because the laws governing intellectual property were seen to grant a legal monopoly to the owner of intellectual property, their purposes were thought to be fundamentally at odds with those of the antitrust laws. Sometimes judges came to that conclusion by confusing the legal monopoly conferred by patent law over a single invention with the economic monopoly of a relevant market that triggers antitrust scrutiny. As a result, for much of the twentieth century, courts relied upon antitrust law to limit the protection afforded the owners of intellectual property.

"[T]he aims and objectives of patent and antitrust laws may seem, at first glance, wholly at odds. However, the two bodies of law are actually complementary, as both are aimed at encouraging innovation, industry and competition."

ATARI GAMES CORP. V. NINTENDO OF AMERICA, INC.,
897 F.2d 1572, 1576 (Fed. Cir. 1990)

Typical was the willingness to find unlawfulness in certain kinds of patent licensing. In one case the Supreme Court, equating patent protection with economic monopoly, held that a patent created an unlawful tying arrangement. Thus, the Court found the practice of requiring licensees of salt-processing machines to purchase salt from the licensor unlawful—without considering how many other brands of machines were available, what percentage of the market was controlled by the patent holder, or whether other competing processes existed.

The Supreme Court's reasoning in that case is now widely recognized as flawed. Although a patent does create a legal monopoly, it does not necessarily create a monopoly in the economic sense. Certainly, the patent holder can prevent others from using the patented process; the patent holder cannot, however, prevent others from developing and marketing competing processes that may be adequate or even superior substitutes—thus depriving the patent holder of any shadow of market power.

But that historical conflict still influences cases in court. Ancient precedent still exists in the casebooks and has yet to be explicitly overruled. Although academics have written insightful commentary and the federal enforcement agencies issued useful intellectual property guidelines in 1995, the problem still facing a trial judge is precisely how to determine and define the point at which efforts to protect intellectual property cease being beneficial and instead become detrimental to consumers.

As the twenty-first century dawned, with the world's leading economies increasingly reliant on burgeoning high-technology industries, many of them firmly built on intellectual property of all kinds, a new controversy has boiled up in courtrooms and on op-ed pages. The antitrust laws were enacted in an economy dominated by heavy "smokestack" industries with their emphasis on size and geographic sweep. But are those laws really suitable for the dynamic, innovation-based industries of the new economy, industries such as communications, pharmaceuticals, computer hardware and software, and all the others where intellectual property is key?

Antitrust critics argue that the speed of market transition renders the notion of barriers to entry meaningless and antitrust enforcement therefore superfluous. They point to the need for collaborative effort to fund massive research and development projects and wonder whether the Sherman Act, with its historic concern about competitor collaborations, impedes important innovation. Finally, they cite the new industries characterized by network efficiencies—industries like the computer software industry or certain communications sectors where the number of users determines the value of a product and where the format that gains favor often results in monopoly—and ask whether an antimonopoly enforcement effort is beside the point or even harmful. Now that VHS has swamped the Betamax format for videotapes or the Microsoft operating system towers over rivals, the price of vigorous antitrust enforcement must, some argue, lead to real consumer welfare losses. Competitive incentives of dominant firms hoping to avoid enforcement action will inevitably be dulled. And if they are sued and lose, the remedies of mandated access or, worse, breakup—even if practical—can destroy the benefits of efficient technology.

But the dilemma, though difficult, is more apparent than real. Unless one is prepared to endorse an antitrust exemption for any industry with a plausible claim to being high-tech—something not even the most doctrinaire free marketeers are ready to support—the real question is not whether antitrust applies to the new economy, but how.

The antitrust laws have always contained the flexibility to take into account the attributes of specialized industries in the context of particular cases—high-tech industries are no exception. For instance, the same Sherman Act language that makes price-fixing a criminal offense treats research and development joint ventures with great leniency. Monopoly achieved by superior technology or as the result of network effects is not in itself an antitrust violation. In short, facts matter.

Nor are speed and technological complexity arguments for staying the hand of antitrust enforcement officials; instead, they counsel the need for greater skill and efficiency in enforcement efforts and warn of greater challenges to prosecutorial discretion. No doubt the new technology presents very difficult questions to our courts, not to mention juries, and our enforcement agencies: understanding the technology, where it is heading, and the economic significance of those facts is a daunting enough challenge. But understanding all of that, reaching the correct judgment, and, where necessary, ordering a correct remedy within a relevant time frame and before the technological map changes beyond recognition are a fundamental but unavoidable challenge to our legal system. That challenge existed long before "new economy" industries appeared on the scene and has been successfully met in the great majority of antitrust cases.

Analysis of Antitrust Claims

As readers will have come to expect, analysis of antitrust claims involving intellectual property first asks what is the relevant market. Three possible markets are at issue: the market for the product; the technology, or intellectual property, market; and finally, the market for research and development in a particular field, sometimes called the innovation market.

Defining the traditional product market, or the market for goods, is uncontroversial. Acquisition of intellectual property from a competitor may diminish competition in the product market by removing a firm's ability to produce a good that is a close substitute for that of the acquirer; licensing arrangements can unduly reduce the licensee's ability to sell products within certain territories or for certain purposes.

The intellectual property market presents more difficult problems. Firms compete in the transfer, licensing, or use of intellectual property. Thus, acquisitions or licensing in those markets might well reduce competition in the market for technology. The market can be analyzed separately from the product market whenever technology is marketed apart from the product.

More controversially, enforcement agencies and some commentators have begun to speak of a separate market for research and development. The thought is that conduct that diminishes competition in research and development, even though no intellectual property has yet been developed, is itself harmful to competition. For example, the Federal Trade Commission has challenged a merger on the grounds that it would reduce competition in the research and development market for gene therapies. On the basis of the merger's putative effect of reducing competition in an innovation market, the commission required that the merging entity grant nonexclusive licenses to technology necessary to the development of products that did not yet exist. However controversial that may now seem, fast-paced innovation in high-technology industries and a public policy that seeks to maintain that pace ensure that separate innovation markets will be examined with increasing frequency in the future.

With the relevant markets selected, the mode of analysis is by now familiar. Most claims will be analyzed under the rule of reason. The competitive benefit of a patent licensing agreement will be weighed against its burden on competition, and the question asked whether similar benefit could be attained by means that are significantly less restrictive. How exhaustive that analysis is and whether relevant markets are always formally and rigorously defined depend upon the circumstances of the case. Mergers involving intellectual property will be analyzed to determine whether the injury to competition is outweighed by procompetitive effects and efficiencies.

Certain conduct, such as resale price-fixing or tying, will receive somewhat less generous treatment. Behavior that almost always reduces competition and is unrelated to any efficiency justification will receive cursory review with a presumption of illegality. Under that standard, the enforcement agency makes only a limited examination to search out some plausible justification for the conduct that would lessen the anticompetitive impact. Finding none, however, the agency will proceed to challenge the conduct under the per se rule.

The usual forms of conduct that are per se illegal in other antitrust contexts are treated similarly in the field of intellectual property. Naked horizontal price-fixing and market allocation, for instance, will be deemed per se illegal there, as elsewhere, regardless of any asserted procompetitive effect.

At the other end of the spectrum, the guidelines issued by the Department of Justice and the Federal Trade Commission have created a small "safety zone" in which the enforcement agencies will not scrutinize conduct. First, the conduct cannot be of a kind normally afforded per se treatment. Second, the licensor and the licensee must collectively account for less than 20 percent of the relevant market affected by the restraint. If those two criteria are satisfied, the enforcement agencies will not look further. The safe-harbor provisions, however, apply only to licensing arrangements and the enforcement of intellectual property rights, not to the acquisition of intellectual property, either by way of securing an exclusive license or outright purchase.

Importantly, the analysis and results of antitrust challenges to specific practices involving intellectual property are likely to be the same irrespective of the nature of the intellectual property—patents, trademarks, copyrights, or trade secrets.

Acquisition of Intellectual Property Rights

Generally, the acquisition of intellectual property rights raises few antitrust concerns. Indeed, the transferability of a patent may be necessary to bring the new invention to the commercial market. Even obtaining a patent through fraud on the Patent Office—intentional misrepresentation without which the patent would not have been issued—is not itself a violation of the antitrust laws, although it may form the basis for an action seeking cancellation of the patent. Thus, in the vast majority of cases the transfer of intellectual property rights is routine.

It is another matter when a transfer of intellectual property forms a critical element in a scheme to monopolize a relevant market or to restrain trade. For instance, a court has found that the acquisition of every relevant patent in the field for the purpose of excluding competition constitutes a violation of Section 2 of the Sherman Act. Likewise, if the effort to enforce a patent procured by fraud is part of a scheme to monopolize or to attempt to monopolize, a suit for infringement is likely to be met by a counterclaim alleging a violation of Section 2 of the Sherman Act. But those are the rare cases; ordinarily, intellectual property rights are transferred every day without triggering antitrust scrutiny.

Enforcement of Intellectual Property Rights

Intellectual property rights are enforced by suits for unlawful infringement. In an infringement suit, antitrust issues are routinely raised by way of counterclaim by the alleged infringer. If successful, the party asserting the claim may receive monetary damages. Any decision to sue for infringement must take into account the likelihood and the seriousness of an antitrust counterclaim by return mail.

Such claims may or may not include the infringement suit as an element of the alleged antitrust violation. An antitrust counterclaim may be based entirely upon anticompetitive acts committed by the patentee outside of the infringement suit. In essence, the actions for monopolization, tying, and other antitrust violations, discussed in previous chapters, are similarly actionable as counterclaims in patent infringement suits. For example, in an action for infringement of the plaintiff's patent on gyratory crushers (used by mining companies to crush rock), the defendant counterclaimed that the plaintiff's act of forcing licensees also to purchase its unpatented epoxy resin constituted an illegal tying arrangement in violation of Section 1 of the Sherman Act. Although such an antitrust suit may be brought separately, packaging it as a counterclaim provides an alleged infringer with a powerful leveraging tool to help dispose of the infringement claim.

Other antitrust counterclaims, asserted only when a patentee chooses to bring an infringement action, allege that the infringement action itself is an integral part of an antitrust violation. Such a claim requires a demonstration that the patentee brought the infringement action in bad faith: either the intellectual property was obtained by fraud or the infringement action is objectively baseless.

"[T]he right of a patentee afforded by patent law to assert that a competitor is engaged in wrongful conduct with respect to the patent requires that a complaining competitor allege and prove bad faith for each such claim."

ZENITH ELECTRONICS CORP. V. EXZEC INC.,
182 F.3d 1340, 1355 (Fed. Cir. 1999)

A lawsuit claiming infringement is objectively baseless when there can be no reasonable expectation of success on the merits. Such sham litigation attempting to employ the governmental process to interfere directly with a competitor's business relationships could result in a finding of liability.

Although commonly pled, bad faith and sham litigation counterclaims rarely result in damage awards for the asserting party. That is true even when the asserting party can demonstrate a patentee's acquisition of its patent by fraud or its bringing of an objectively baseless infringement action. The important requirement—demonstrating that a patentee has market power in the relevant market—still poses a significant hurdle for many antitrust claimants.

That difficulty has spurred a new development in patent infringement litigation whereby infringement defendants, in certain circumstances, may bring state or federal "unfair competition" claims in conjunction with or instead of antitrust counterclaims. Such claims are based not on the antitrust laws, but instead on unfair competition principles protected by state laws (discussed more fully in chapter 11) and federal laws such as the Lanham Act.

Importantly, such "unfair competition" claims do not require proof of a patentee's market power nor of the other requirements necessary to sustain an antitrust violation. But they do still require a finding that the infringement action was brought in bad faith. "Unfair competition" claims also allow for the recovery of monetary damages. As a result, such claims are becoming increasingly attractive to alleged infringers that may not be able otherwise to succeed in bringing an antitrust counterclaim.

Closely related to the antitrust counterclaims asserted in infringement actions is the affirmative defense based on the patent misuse doctrine. In essence, the defense is that the patent alleged to have been infringed has been "misused" or used in a way that violates the patent laws, the antitrust laws, or some related legal policy. Although the misuse doctrine typically relies on the patent under scrutiny having been used anticompetitively—for instance, in connection with the fixing of the price at which patented goods may be resold to the public—the doctrine does not require that the conduct actually be an antitrust violation. It may instead be that the conduct only meets the lower standard of seeming anticompetitive—although the courts have been raising the standard in recent years. The effect of that important distinction, however, is that a successfully asserted misuse defense only renders the patent unenforceable against the party asserting the defense; it does not provide for monetary damages. Thus, it is helpful to think of antitrust law and the patent misuse doctrine as overlapping without being identical.

Just as the bringing of a patent infringement suit may result in antitrust scrutiny, so too may the settlement of infringement suits or attempts at preventing a party from enforcing its intellectual property rights. Licensing and pooling arrangements, discussed in detail later in this chapter, are common means used to settle infringement suits whereby parties agree to cross-license competing patents. Those arrangements can create efficiencies through the integration of complementary components of production that might otherwise be impeded by blocking patents (or patents that are all necessary elements in the manufacture of a single specific product). Such arrangements are not, however, immune from antitrust scrutiny. Where such arrangements are entered into to avoid a finding that both parties' patents are invalid or to enhance the parties' market positions with respect to unlicensed competitors, violations of the antitrust laws may be found. For example, a plaintiff successfully alleged that an infringement settlement between two prescription drug manufacturers violated Sections 1 and 2 of the Sherman Act, where one company paid the other $40 million in exchange for its agreement to postpone the sale of its competing, generic version of the patented drug in dispute to firms in the United States.

Similarly, the antitrust agencies have suggested that an antitrust violation may also arise where a party attempts to coerce a patentee not to enforce its intellectual property rights against it. That was the essence of the recent Federal Trade Commission action against Intel Corporation. In that action, the commission alleged that Intel violated Section 5 of the Federal Trade Commission Act by withholding, or threatening to withhold, vital technical information concerning general-purpose microprocessors from certain customers to coerce them into dropping their existing infringement suits against Intel and instead licensing their intellectual property to Intel. The case was settled with an FTC order prohibiting Intel from withholding advance technical information from a customer who had asserted intellectual property rights against Intel if that customer were receiving such information from Intel at the time of the dispute.

If there is a general rule of thumb that may be gleaned from the case law concerning how a patentee may enforce its rights without running afoul of the antitrust laws, it would simply be this: an intellectual property owner may protect its invention by enforcing its rights as a shield against infringers but, conversely, may not use its power to enforce those rights as a sword to eliminate competition unfairly.

Licensing

Having obtained a patent grant, and with it the concomitant right to exclude others from making, using, or selling the covered invention, a patentee may seek to profit from its patent for financial, business, or personal gain. It is this interest in profiting from the invention that drives a patentee to license its patent to others.

Licensing arrangements, like other agreements involving intellectual property, are typically procompetitive because they increase the rate of diffusion of new technology. In those rare situations in which monopolization or restraint of trade concerns arise, however, license agreements may be subjected to antitrust scrutiny. Under evolving precedent and pursuant to the enforcement agencies' guidelines, most such cases involve evaluation of the licensing arrangements under the rule of reason. The narrow exception for per se treatment would be limited to licensing arrangements that are the incidental instruments to implement conspiracies among competitors to fix prices, divide markets, or engage in other naked restraints of trade.

In analyzing intellectual property licenses under the antitrust laws, characterization is critically important. Recall from earlier chapters that somewhat different and tougher rules apply to relationships between competitors than to those between sellers and customers. There is no doubt that a patent license between competitors has both horizontal and vertical aspects. A patent licensing agreement between competitors is considered primarily horizontal if it is used to implement collusive behavior such as a market allocation or price-fixing scheme. On the other hand, a licensing arrangement takes on a more vertical character when it is between firms that have a complementary relationship, for instance, an agreement between a research and development company, on the one hand, and a manufacturer on the other.

Another point of distinction in the analysis of licenses is whether they are exclusive or nonexclusive. On the one hand, a patent owner may grant a party an exclusive license allowing the licensee to enforce the rights of the patent as if it were the patent holder. Because of the level of control conferred upon the licensee, such licenses are commonly negotiated for higher royalty rates. On the other hand, a patent owner may choose to license to multiple licensees by negotiating nonexclusive license agreements, which allow the licensee to use or manufacture the patented invention but not enforce the patent right against infringers. Such nonexclusive licenses are often negotiated for significantly lower royalty rates.

A patent licensing agreement is lawful even if it is exclusive; indeed, the Patent Act expressly provides for the transfer of an exclusive right to practice a patent. An exclusive patent license raises antitrust concerns only when a merger would raise concerns, as, for example, when the licensor and the licensee are either actual or potential competitors of one another. Nonexclusive licenses are generally far safer but may also raise antitrust concerns, for example, when circumstances suggest that, in practice, they are acting as exclusive licenses that have an anticompetitive effect. For example, in 1994, the Department of Justice alleged that a nonexclusive license granted to the leading producer of household insecticides was actually an exclusive license that protected the defendant's dominance of the U.S. market against a foreign competitor. The government alleged that the licensor was a potential new entrant into the household insecticide market and, instead of entering the market, the licensor gave the licensee effectively exclusive control of its patented technology and agreed to refuse all other licensing offers.

Beyond the fact of the license itself, any of the central terms of the license may have antitrust significance. Consider, for instance, the royalty to be paid. In general, a patent owner may charge as high a royalty as the market will bear. Royalties are typically calculated on the basis of sales of the patented product. But where the royalty rate is calculated on some other basis unrelated to the utilization of the patent, it can be unlawful as an instance of patent misuse. In its first case against Microsoft, the government challenged the software giant's practice of requiring a license fee for each computer a licensee manufactured, regardless of whether Microsoft's software was installed. By requiring what were in effect double license fees—one to Microsoft and another to the company whose software was actually used—Microsoft had erected an unjustified barrier in the path of its competitors.

The license agreement may also attempt to set the price at which the product manufactured by the licensee can be sold. That practice is commonly referred to as resale price maintenance. The rationale is that the licensor, were it to keep the right to manufacture to itself, could charge a monopoly price. That same logic is also normally held to support a patent holder's ability to set both maximum and minimum resale prices.

But such limited resale price maintenance is fraught with difficulty. The Supreme Court decision approving it (*United States v. General Electric Co.,* 272 U.S. 476 (1926)) is aged and has been nearly overruled on several occasions. Antitrust Division officials over the years have targeted it, so far unsuccessfully, for the junk heap. Even in its somewhat ragged state, it has been sharply limited. Price restrictions may not be imposed on a licensee's sale of a patented product where the licensor only sold the licensee an unpatented product.

Likewise, the licensor who manufactures and sells the patented product is prohibited from trying to control, through a license to sell but not manufacture, the price of that product's resale.

So resale price maintenance in the intellectual property area, as elsewhere, is looked at with great suspicion. Any type of price restriction in a license agreement runs the risk of encountering hostile enforcement agency scrutiny. Still, patent holders can count on at least a few relatively clear rules. First, it seems clear that the pricing provisions may not apply to unpatented products, and in addition the courts have held that the licensor may not reach out further to control the prices charged by customers of the licensee. Finally, courts have generally condemned license agreements that require a royalty after the supporting patent has expired.

Each one of those results is explained by an effort to walk the fine line of giving the patent owner the full benefits of the patent, but at the same time confining those benefits as far as practical to the product or process covered by the patent. That same tension is seen in the rule that the patent holder may restrict the licensee's sales to a given territory, even if it is a direct competitor of the licensee, or may limit sales of the patented product to specified customer classes. And "field of use" restrictions, where a patent owner restricts the scope of the license to specified products or uses, are also generally lawful. On the same theory, courts have also sustained the ability of the licensor to limit the quantity of the patented product manufactured under the license.

There is, of course, a limit. Where what is at issue is not so much the licensing of a significant patent as it is the division of a marketing territory or the allocation of customers, as would be indicated by weak patents or patents of trivial importance, then the per se rule will be applied. For example, an agreement between two Georgia bar review companies, where one company granted an exclusive copyright license to the other in exchange for an assurance that the licensee would not compete in any markets outside Georgia, was condemned under the per se rule as a naked horizontal market division scheme.

Sometimes, a licensing arrangement contains a grant-back provision, in which a patentee licenses a patent but only on the condition that a licensee's future innovation on the patent is transferred back to the original licensee. Only where the grant-back provision might have the net effect of chilling innovation will the courts intervene to overturn the license. Were the grant-back requirement exclusive, for instance, the licensee might feel little temptation to develop the patent, inasmuch as it would lose control of the innovation. In such a case, an antitrust violation might well be found.

Intellectual property licenses sometimes contain terms designed to give the licensor some priority over its competitors in the licensee's purchasing patterns. There may be an effort to mandate an exclusive dealing relationship, or a license can be written to include a tying arrangement (each is discussed more fully in chapter nine).

Exclusive dealing involving intellectual property, as elsewhere, may be benign if it has no significant anticompetitive effects. On the other hand, when enforced by a licensor with substantial market power for a lengthy term having adverse competitive effects, exclusive dealing arrangements will be condemned. The first *Microsoft* case, discussed above, is such an example.

On occasion, a licensor may attempt to incorporate a tying arrangement into a licensing agreement seeking to force a licensee to purchase an unpatented or unwanted article in exchange for the opportunity to license its patented product. Courts traditionally presumed that a patent or copyright itself conferred adequate market power to satisfy that aspect of tying arrangement analysis. That conclusion is no longer automatic. Today, the existence of intellectual property is one step along the road to showing a tying arrangement, but the rest of the proof must follow. Even then, at least under the intellectual property guidelines, the entire arrangement will be subjected to what is in effect a rule-of-reason analysis.

The same result follows in connection with licensing a group of related patents as a single package, a practice commonly referred to as package licensing. Package licensing may be construed as an illegal tying arrangement.

A good demonstration of many of those principles is the government's most recent case against Microsoft. There the government alleged that Microsoft's practice of bundling its largely unpopular Internet browser with its hugely successful operating system constituted an illegal tying arrangement. Microsoft countered that there could be no tie because there was only one product on offer—an operating system with an integrated browser. After hearing the evidence, the trial court found that browsers and operating systems are distinguishable in the eyes of buyers and that Microsoft's integration of the two was motivated less by technical necessity or business efficiency than by a "deliberate and purposeful choice to quell incipient competition." Accordingly, after finding market power and a not insubstantial foreclosure effect, the court found that tying arrangement a violation of the Sherman Act.

On appeal, the finding of a violation based on per se analysis was set aside and the tying allegation remanded to the trial court. Because the antitrust law had so little experience with bundling software and functionality, the appellate court was insistent that at least this "first up-close look" at technological integration involving platform software be conducted with rule-of-reason flexibility.

Outside traditional licensing arrangements, multiple patent owners in a common industry may engage in more complicated licensing arrangements commonly referred to as patent pools. Patent holders will often enter into patent pools in an effort to alleviate licensing problems for a particular product that are caused by blocking patents or industry standards.

Patent pools are analyzed under the rule of reason, and most are found legal. But once again, exclusivity can trigger per se treatment. The true purpose of the patent pool will turn out to be dispositive. Where two firms hold blocking patents, the cross-licensing of the blocking patents would seem to be entirely legitimate; in the absence of such cross-licensing, progress would be stymied. Similarly, patent pools that are created to avoid licensing difficulties inherent in conforming with new industry standards will not normally create antitrust problems, where those patents involved are essential in conforming with the standard. For instance, in 1998, the Department of Justice issued a business review letter that summarily confirmed that there were no potential antitrust problems with a patent pooling arrangement among owners of numerous patents essential in the manufacture of products that comply with DVD–format industry standards.

Furthermore, the formation of a patent pool does not automatically require members to admit every competitor. A different rule applies, however, if the pool creates market power and access would be necessary to compete in the market.

Even in industries where licensing is commonplace, a patent owner may always unilaterally refuse to license its patent. That refusal is judged to be within the grant of the patent and therefore not an antitrust violation, even where the patent owner has monopoly power in a relevant market that includes the patented product. As discussed earlier in this chapter, however, a refusal to license that is the product of an agreement between competitors stands on a very different footing and will likely receive antitrust scrutiny.

It may already be obvious that the competitive concerns with patents and their licenses are similar to those involving other forms of intellectual property, such as trade secrets. It should also be obvious that the courts, when dealing with intellectual property, strive to accord the owner a virtually absolute right to use and dispose of his property as he sees fit, subject only to a prohibition on using that right to mask a restraint of trade or as a crucial component of a scheme to monopolize.

Finally, intellectual property rights can be used in such a way as to control an essential input required for competition in a market, sometimes called a bottleneck. The Microsoft operating system could be described as a bottleneck; the Intel control over the general purpose computer processor market may be another. Where an intellectual property bottleneck has been brought into being by the misuse of intellectual property rights, mandatory licensing may be ordered if necessary to destroy the bottleneck and if future innovation will not as a result be unnecessarily restrained.

ELEVEN

Complementary Regimes

To this point we have spoken of federal antitrust law, which may be enforced by federal authorities and state attorneys general, and we have touched lightly on the subject of private plaintiffs. The interested observer should be aware, however, of regimes of antitrust law that are quite separate from the federal law. Specifically, business people must be knowledgeable about state antitrust enforcement. A few additional words about the private treble damage remedy are also in order because of its importance—and unpredictability.

State Antitrust Enforcement

Twenty-one states had their own antitrust laws on the books by the time of the passage of the Sherman Act in 1890. Now, virtually every state has its own antitrust law. Each state antitrust law is enforced by the state attorney general, whose antitrust enforcement staff may vary from fifty or so lawyers down to one or two part-timers. Most states and the District of Columbia have instituted criminal penalties for violation of those laws; fines are common, but imprisonment is quite rare. Civil penalties are a part of most states' enforcement arsenals, and many state antitrust laws also provide for private actions with recoveries of up to treble damages. That state enforcement complement to the federal effort presents violators with the specter of multiple suits brought to recover damages as well as civil penalties and criminal fines. State antitrust cases may be filed in the state court system, or allegations of state antitrust law violations may be filed as part of larger federal cases in a federal court.

In federal court a state will sue to collect damages that it suffered in its capacity as the direct purchaser of the product at issue. A state can also institute federal class-action suits, and under a special provision of federal law, the state may file suit as *parens patriae*—literally, as father of the country—to recover damages for injuries to state residents. State attorneys general communicate with one another on antitrust matters, and in matters of nationwide scope they frequently cooperate by pooling resources and trading investigative information. A Multistate Antitrust Task Force now meets several times a year to discuss litigation matters, to debate legislative issues, and, on occasion, to establish antitrust policy guidelines. As with similar federal efforts, the states' guidelines on vertical restraints and on merger enforcement are meant to encapsulate the states' antitrust philosophy and enforcement policy in those areas.

Since state antitrust laws are very similar to federal antitrust laws, much of what we have said about the substance of the federal antitrust laws in earlier chapters also applies to the state antitrust laws. Indeed, many state antitrust statutes include a provision to the effect that the state law is to be interpreted consistently with the federal law.

But state laws are not identical to the federal laws. Some states omit some federal counterparts, particularly the antimerger prohibitions. Other states have statutes for which no federal counterpart exists. A typical and widespread example is an unfair sales prohibition, which generally bars certain kinds of discounts. The practical effect of those kinds of statutes is to make many forms of price competition more difficult. Frequently, those unfair sales provisions are enforced as part of the state antitrust law, but their theme and direction are precisely contrary to federal antitrust policy.

Even if the text of the laws is very much the same, enforcement priorities of state attorneys general may differ from those of the federal authorities. Although it is difficult to generalize, state attorneys general are frequently interested in elective advancement. As a result, their enforcement programs may be very different from those of the antitrust officials who control the Antitrust Division or the Federal Trade Commission, very few of whom have political ambitions. State enforcement may be more solicitous of small business and thus more inclined to put enforcement resources into, for instance, cases dealing with vertical arrangements, which are of secondary importance in federal enforcement plans.

Relationships between federal and state antitrust authorities ebb and flow over time. On occasions, there have been very sharp differences as the result of doctrinal conflict. At other times, federal and state authorities have acted cooperatively, and indeed on occasion enforcement officials at one level may be seconded to another for special assistance in particular cases. In recent years federal-state relations have been harmonious. An antitrust working group serves as a forum for coordination efforts, including the joint prosecution of cases. Although federal and state enforcement efforts can run in parallel against the same conduct, federal policy generally discourages duplicative enforcement. Particularly in connection with highly localized activity, the Justice Department and the FTC will refer investigations to the appropriate state attorney general.

In the merger area the cooperation between federal and state authorities is particularly close. In recent years, the Justice Department and the FTC announced separate programs to enhance federal-state cooperation in merger investigations. If parties to a merger explicitly consent—and they frequently have a strong incentive to do so—federal authorities will share confidential information with their state enforcement colleagues and will assist the states, if "practicable and desirable," with the analysis of the transaction at issue.

A complicated situation arises when there is a conflict. In those situations in which conduct is subject to detailed regulatory control under federal antitrust decrees, state antitrust enforcement, particularly if it seems headed in a different direction, will be barred. But those cases are still rare, even though they may become more frequent as state attorneys general become more active in the antitrust area. As the frequency of those cases increases, federal courts may yet have to decide that federal authority must have sway. But we are not there yet.

Private Actions

Section 4 of the Clayton Act provides for a private right of action for persons suffering antitrust injury. A suc-

111

cessful plaintiff is entitled to treble damages. The number of private actions in any given year has always greatly exceeded the number brought by the government.

Private antitrust treble damage actions are controversial: should they be permitted at all, and are treble damages the right result? One side argues that elected governments should have the responsibility for making competition policy, rather than private parties appealing to unpredictable juries. The other side counters that the private right of action creates an army of "private attorneys general" to supplement the often limited resources of government, especially in areas of major concern to small businesses. Private actions can take over where the public agencies leave off.

As for the treble damages remedy, those opposing private suits say that the imposition of treble damage claims may lead to frivolous suits. Plaintiffs are aware that treble damage claims can force settlements that may be more cost-efficient to defendants than proceeding with a litigation defense, no matter how well founded. Treble damage awards themselves may lead to overdeterrence; borderline beneficial practices may be passed up for fear of being hit by ruinous antitrust damages.

The judiciary has responded to the possibility of frivolous treble damage claims by limiting the number of permissible antitrust plaintiffs. At least under federal law, "standing" requirements tend to favor customers and competitors as antitrust plaintiffs while disfavoring others with more attenuated relationships. Furthermore, a plaintiff must demonstrate direct "antitrust injury" or risk having the case dismissed. Faced with an implausible or frivolous case, the judiciary is likely to dispose of the case in a summary manner, thereby avoiding the need to slog through lengthy and expensive pretrial and trial proceedings.

An additional level of complexity—and risk for defendants—is introduced when an antitrust plaintiff sues as representative of a class. The class can be all-encompassing: "all airline passengers within a certain period," "all consumers of soft drinks," or "all makers of long-distance telephone calls from a hotel telephone." The definition and certification of a proper class constitute an entirely separate—and somewhat tedious—stage of antitrust litigation, but they remain vitally important because class damages are simply individual damages multiplied by thousands, millions, or more.

TWELVE

International Antitrust Enforcement

Three developments have changed antitrust from a peculiarly American institution into an international one. First, the increased globalization of major businesses has transformed most companies into organizations that buy, sell, and, most important, merge with little regard to national boundaries.

Second, the realization by other countries that competition, rather than state monopolies or private cartels, is a key factor in adding to the wealth of nations has spawned a proliferation of antitrust laws and enforcement agencies, both in individual nations and, in the case of the European Union, at the transnational level.

Third, the deregulation of industries previously regarded as "natural monopolies"—electricity suppliers, gas companies, telecommunications companies, airlines—has increased the role played by antitrust authorities in reviewing mergers and competitive tactics in those industries, many of them characterized by multinational companies.

U.S. Enforcement Abroad

It has, of course, always been the case that American antitrust jurisdiction extends abroad, and there has always been a steady stream of enforcement activity focused on international transactions and conduct by foreign companies that have an effect in the United States. U.S. enforcement authorities, as well as private treble damage plaintiffs, can use the U.S. antitrust laws to challenge conduct that takes place abroad if it significantly affects either consumers in the United States or American export opportunities to foreign countries. That jurisdictional reality exists regardless of whether the conduct is by American firms or foreign businesses.

A conspiracy to boycott the U.S. market, hatched in a Paris hotel room by citizens of several different countries who are directors of marketing for a variety of American and foreign companies, is every bit as subject to U.S. jurisdiction, and indeed criminal treatment, as a similar conspiracy that had its locus in middle America.

In fact, in recent years, worldwide cartels have become a major priority for U.S. enforcement agencies, and the Antitrust Division has increased the resources it devotes to the investigation and prosecution of international cartel activity. Nowadays, one-third of the Antitrust Division's criminal investigations involve international cartel activity. Recent investigations have looked at conduct in very large industries in over thirty-five different countries on four continents.

The results have been unhappy for cartelists. In the five years since 1996, defendants have been fined over $10 million in at least twenty-seven cases. In 1999 the Antitrust Division obtained fines totaling in excess of $1 billion.

Perhaps the most dramatic example of the authorities' increased attention to, and effectiveness against, cartels is provided by the food and feed additives industries. Government investigators, tipped off by an informant and aided by electronic and video surveillance, uncovered a sophisticated and complex conspiracy in which high-level executives (termed *the masters*) held secret meetings throughout the world to agree on the general terms of the conspiracy. Then, lower-level executives (referred to as *the sherpas*) worked out such details as the prices to be charged for citric acid and the precise share of the market allocated to each conspirator, down to one-tenth of a decimal point. Each cartel member exchanged monthly sales figures with the other members, and at year-end companies that had sold more than the conspiracy allowed were required to purchase the excess from other conspirators that had fallen short. The internal corporate slogan of one of the defendant companies, revealed by the company's president on a government surveillance video, summed up those corporations' attitudes to competition in the marketplace: "Our competitors are our friends. Our customers are the enemy."

The food and feed additives investigation yielded an unprecedented level of fines: one conspirator alone paid a $100 million fine. Subsequent investigations, however, have produced corporate fines that dwarf that figure. In a recent Justice Department investigation of price-fixing in the international vitamin market, fines reached as high as $500 million for one corporate defendant and $225 million for another.

Fines are not the only penalty faced by cartelists. Perhaps even more worrying to corporate executives who participate in those schemes is the increased prospect of jail time. For example, in the vitamins investigation, four former executives—two Swiss nationals and two German nationals—agreed to plead guilty, pay criminal fines, and serve time in U.S. prisons.

The threat of jail sentences has combined with the recent changes in the Antitrust Division's corporate leniency program to increase the number of companies volunteering to cooperate with the division in its investigations and prosecutions. The division is willing to consider corporate amnesty and amnesty for individual employees involved in conspiracies, even if an investigation is already underway, if those who seek the protection offer useful and new information that assists the investigators.

Any executive availing himself of that program must keep in mind that information provided to one antitrust authority may, pursuant to an ever growing network of cooperation agreements, be made available to foreign antitrust authorities. By cooperating with U.S. antitrust authorities, a corporation may proffer evidence that the U.S. Department of Justice may exchange, for example, with Canadian authorities, and such information could then be used in a prosecution by the Canadian Competition Bureau.

The law also permits antitrust challenge to foreigners' conduct that takes place entirely abroad if the effect impedes, in any significant way, the efforts of American companies to export goods into foreign markets. For instance, as the 1995 Antitrust Enforcement Guidelines for International Operations point out, U.S. authorities will challenge agreements by foreign producers, almost all of whom have some assets in America, to attempt to prevent the distribution of a

U.S. company's exports to the producer's country. Likewise, U.S. authorities will attack an agreement by foreign manufacturers on industry standards that are intended to exclude U.S. technology.

There are, of course, differences in how the antitrust laws approach cases with an international dimension, even if the substance of the law is very much the same. Because such litigation can trigger heated jurisdictional disputes with other countries that may feel that their law rather than U.S. antitrust law should regulate the conduct, the Justice Department will not take action reflexively to challenge such conduct without carefully considering the international implications. For example, the department will assess how serious the impact of the anticompetitive conduct is in the United States, whether any other country is likely to challenge the conduct under its own law, and whether there are important American policy interests that can be vindicated only by a U.S. government suit. The Justice Department, perhaps in conjunction with the State Department, will thoroughly review all those questions.

Even so, and despite the increased willingness of enforcement authorities of other nations to cooperate with our Antitrust Division, not every country is thrilled to have its citizens hailed into an American courtroom. Some countries, notably several leading members of the British Commonwealth, have enacted a variety of blocking statutes that can be used in a narrow category of cases to frustrate U.S. jurisdiction. Others have gone so far as to make the gathering of evidence in connection with an antitrust case a violation of their criminal law.

Most of those disputes can be avoided in one of three ways. First, the enforcement agencies can exercise self-discipline in conducting the investigation or framing the legal challenge. Second, the courts have the power to deal with that narrow category of cases that cause international tension. For instance, it is quite clear that courts will not apply the U.S. antitrust laws to make conduct unlawful if it has been compelled by a foreign government and occurs outside the United States. Finally, foreigners sometimes have the option of avoiding the jurisdiction: a subpoena for testimony before an antitrust grand jury is ineffective as long as the object of the subpoena is willing to remain outside the United States and is certain he will never find himself on an airplane with engine trouble forced to land, say, at Kennedy Airport.

To help sort through the complicated threads of the problem of international antitrust jurisdiction, the Justice Department has over the years promulgated antitrust guidelines that reflect its approach to international operations. Most recently, the 1995 Antitrust Enforcement Guidelines for International Operations confirm the determination of the department to continue its broad international enforcement of U.S. antitrust laws. At the same time, the guidelines set out various limiting factors designed to avoid unnecessary conflict. The 1995 guidelines rehearse the traditional criteria that the department will take into account, including the nationality of the persons involved and the extent of the effect of a foreign firm's conduct on U.S. consumers or markets. But the guidelines add two additional significant factors—the effect of U.S. enforcement action on foreign antitrust enforcement activities and the effectiveness of foreign antitrust enforcement in eliminating the anticompetitive conduct. Where the bringing of an action by U.S. authorities might interfere with the objectives of proceedings brought by foreign antitrust authorities, the Americans will stay their hand. That demonstrates that the U.S. government increasingly recognizes the importance and effectiveness of international enforcement of the antitrust laws and wishes to exercise its own jurisdiction in such a way as to build the alliance, rather than to cause competition—or even antagonism—among the world's competition authorities.

European Union Enforcement

The leading antitrust enforcement authority in Europe is the European Commission, headquartered in Brussels. The European Commission is responsible for enforcing the EU antitrust laws under the EC Treaty, successor to the Treaty of Rome. (Relevant excerpts of the EC treaty are set out in appendix C.) Analysis of enforcement results reveals a narrow substantive difference between EU and U.S. practice. U.S. statutes and practices are more focused on constraining activities shown to harm competition, in the belief that, left unencumbered, competition is in the public interest. The European Union, in contrast, also considers its goal of integrating the separate national economies. Indeed, a commissioner in charge of antitrust enforcement in Brussels has stated that competition policy is "not an end in itself" but instead is designed to achieve the goals of the EC Treaty, including growth of the single market together with its social and environmental dimension and its formal industrial policy.

Restrictive Agreements. Even so, the EU law on the books closely resembles U.S. antitrust law. Very much like Section 1 of the Sherman Act, Article 81 of the EC Treaty prohibits restrictive agreements. As with the Sherman Act, the special enforcement focus is on price-fixing, market division, output limitations, and collective boycotts. And also, as with the Sherman Act's rule of reason, the actual practice of the European Commission has been to adopt a somewhat more permissive attitude toward horizontal arrangements that seem less restrictive, either because they promote efficiency or because they affect a relatively insignificant portion of the market. Note, however, that of late the commission has more closely scrutinized the activities of trade associations and levied heavy fines against those found to be engaged in price-fixing and cartel behavior.

"The following shall be prohibited as incompatible with the common market: all agreements . . . which may affect trade between Member States and which have as their object or effect the prevention, restriction, or distortion of competition."

EC TREATY, ART. 81 (1)

Vertical restrictions likewise come within Article 81. Indeed, because of the special concern for market integration, any territorial restrictions are subject to strict scrutiny. The same sensitivity has influenced the commission in its analysis of restrictive clauses in agreements involving intellectual property rights. Any provision of such agreements that has the effect of segmenting the EU economy will likely be found unlawful. Thus, export bans, exclusive grant-back provisions, and expansive exclusive licenses have been prohibited.

Refusals to deal or exclusive supply contracts have typically been found to be a violation in the presence of dominant position. A market share in excess of 50 percent may be taken as persuasive evidence of the existence of such a position. Also, if a company, because of either market structure or its conduct, is able to act as if it were effectively independent of its competition, the commission will almost certainly find the requisite dominance.

On occasion, after investigation, the commission will elect not to proceed against a particular form of conduct; that is termed a "negative clearance." But the commission also has a power not granted to its American counterparts: it can determine that particular conduct should be exempt for a limited period from the provisions of Article 81, on either an individual or a block basis. If specific conduct satisfies the conditions spelled out in Article 81—that is, it promotes technical or economic progress, the benefits of which are shared by consumers, and the restraints are the least restrictive alternatives—the commission will issue an individual exemption. Block exemptions for certain categories of agreements are appropriate when the commission has determined from its experience that they are, on balance, probably not anticompetitive. Regulations introduced in June 2000 expand the scope of block exemptions to include selective distribution agreements and all vertical agreements in which the supplier's market share does not exceed 30 percent.

In response to an ever increasing desire of corporations to collaborate with other participants in the marketplace, the European Commission recently issued draft guidelines for the analysis of those collaborations' compatibility with Article 81 of the EC Treaty. Similar to the U.S. authorities' joint venture guidelines, the European guidelines provide broad guidance on the dos and don'ts of competitor collaborations; they offer, for example, several broad categories in which the commission may exempt collaborations from scrutiny. For example, vertical distribution agreements or companies collaborating on R&D, standardization, or environmental issues may qualify for an exemption from the provisions of Article 81. Accompanying the new guidelines were redrafts of the regulations concerning block exemptions that were designed to make such exemptions more accessible to businesses. The implementation of those new guidelines, of course, will be the true test of their usefulness to the business community.

Market Power. Article 82, the EU counterpart of Section 2 of the Sherman Act, prohibits the "abuse . . . of a dominant position." The assessment of a dominant position begins, as does the Sherman Act's examination of monopolization, with a definition of the relevant product market and geographic market, and an analysis of the firm's market share. In practice, EU authorities tend to prefer much narrower market definitions than their U.S. counterparts, a convention that results in findings of higher market shares, and to give more weight to purely structural tests than do U.S. authorities.

As noted above, a market share in excess of 50 percent may be taken as evidence of dominance, which is generally taken to mean an ability to behave to an appreciable extent independently of competitors and customers. As a general rule, a market share exceeding

50 percent is almost conclusive proof of dominance in the relevant market, and a share less than 25 percent is not likely to be sufficient.

But dominance is not prohibited under Article 82, which proscribes only the abuse of that position. Such abuse includes a range of practices, from stifling innovation to imposing unfair trading conditions and discriminating against customers in a way that places them at a competitive disadvantage.

"Any abuse . . . of a dominant position within the common market . . . shall be prohibited."
                                        EC TREATY, ART. 82

Mergers. Interestingly, the terms of the EC Treaty make no special provision for dealing with mergers and acquisitions. For many years the commission used Article 82 to analyze whether a dominant company had abused its position by acquiring a competitor. The Merger Control Regulation applies to mergers of companies that together have approximately $4 billion of worldwide revenue with each having approximately $210 million of revenue within the European Union or, though slightly smaller, meet lower financial thresholds in at least three member states. Once the thresholds are met, the merging parties are required to file a notification so that the commission can begin its analysis of competitive effect. In the meantime, the national merger laws of any affected countries within the European Union are preempted.

The Merger Control Regulation begins with the dominance concept from Article 82 and moves on to examine the proscribed anticompetitive effect.

Although both Section 7 of the Clayton Act and the Merger Control Regulation focus on consumer welfare, the latter tends to give somewhat greater attention to competitor foreclosure, for instance, emphasizing the exercise of "portfolio power," and at the same time recognizes more explicitly the desirability of efficiencies.

For some time that willingness to recognize offsets to the possible anticompetitive effects of mergers led to a relatively permissive policy toward mergers that were of sufficient size and multinational scope to come within the EC's purview. That policy seems to have changed. The European Commission has now become one of the stricter merger review authorities and has thwarted proposed combinations in industries ranging from aluminum (Aluminum Ltd. and Pechiney) and truck manufacture (Volvo and Scania) to package tours (Airtours and First Choice) and telecommunications (WorldCom and Sprint) and, most recently, aircraft equipment manufacture and financing (GE and Honeywell). The European Commission considers not only the market power of the new consolidation, but what it calls "collective dominance," the market shares of the merged company and of the remaining participants in the market, to assess the likelihood of anticompetitive parallel behavior.

The newly invigorated merger review process notwithstanding, the great bulk of proposed mergers receive approval. Unfortunately, when the European Commission rejects a merger, there is no swift appeal from its decision, and the transaction very likely will be abandoned.

Joint Ventures. The European Commission's treatment of a joint venture will depend on whether the commission considers the arrangement concentrative or cooperative, a distinction not easily made and less easily described. The gist of the distinction relates to the role the parents play after they establish the joint venture. In a concentrative joint venture, the parents yield up the common parts of their business to the joint venture. A cooperative joint venture is said to exist when, after establishing the joint venture, the parents remain active in the market, perhaps to service house accounts or perhaps to serve existing customers while the joint venture concentrates on new accounts.

Because concentrative joint ventures involve the replacement of two or more parents with a single entity, they are subject to the Merger Control Regulation. Cooperative joint ventures, because they involve coordination among the joint venture and its parents and among the parents, are subject to the anticollusion provisions of Article 81 and will be analyzed according to the new guidelines discussed above.

Penalties. In general, the commission has the power to levy fines and issue cease-and-desist orders. Fines under the EC Treaty may as a practical matter range up to 10 percent of the company's worldwide annual turnover. Those fines may be appealed to the Court of First Instance and then to the European Court of Justice. In an effort to increase the transparency of its calculation of fines, the commission in 1998 issued guidelines on how those fines would be calculated. Under the guidelines, the commission determines the gravity and duration of the infringement and then adjusts upward or downward from that figure on the basis of aggravating or attenuating circumstances relating to the infringement. Repeated infringements or "ringleader" status, for example, will increase a party's fine; passivity in the infringement or cooperation with the commission will lessen the fine. As with the United States, the commission will use its leniency program to reward those who reveal cartels and punish those who conceal them.

Antitrust Enforcement by EU Member States

Most of the member states of the European Union have their own domestic antitrust regimes. The most active enforcement is found in France, Germany, and the United Kingdom, all of which deal with restrictive practices, monopoly, and mergers through a combination of administrative decisions and negotiation. In most countries, the antitrust regimes are evolving in the direction of U.S. and EU policies. In France, the Competition Council has taken an increased interest in market allocation and predatory pricing schemes, and in "artificially low pricing." Indeed, European authorities generally worry more about the ability of large firms to use their deep pockets to engage in predatory pricing than does the Antitrust Division.

In Germany, the Federal Cartel Office recently announced a corporate leniency program, mirroring the U.S. amnesty program, for members of hardcore cartels that are willing to come forward and cooperate. In addition, the German Competition Act was recently amended to bring the law more closely in line with EC competition law. But the German authorities continue to fear that competition from large, aggressive, multiproduct retailers might in some circumstances drive smaller firms from the market, to the long-run detriment of competition and consumers. Partly as a consequence of that fear, partly as a result of evidence that Wal-Mart sold some six products, including milk and sugar, at prices below those it paid to its suppliers, the Federal Cartel Office has found Wal-Mart, which acquired ninety-five stores from two German chains, to be guilty of what might be translated loosely as unfair impairment of competition.

In Great Britain a new competition law came into effect early in 2000, intended to align UK law more closely with Articles 81 and 82 of the EC Treaty. The Office of Fair Trading has been restructured to include a government-appointed management board. The director general of fair trading now has the power to conduct "dawn raids"; to levy fines of up to 10 percent of UK turnover for each year of infringement of the law, with a maximum of three years; and to grant immunity to whistle-blowers and reduced penalties to cooperating parties. Injured third parties can seek damages in the courts.

Proposed mergers that do not have an EU dimension are to be reviewed by the Office of Fair Trading. In those instances in which it fears an anticompetitive impact, the office asks the secretary of state for trade and industry to refer the merger to the Competition Commission (formerly the Monopolies and Mergers Commission). A panel is appointed to review the matter and, if it approves the merger, the deal may go forward. If the panel finds that the merger would operate against the public interest, the secretary of state has the power to reverse the Competition Commission, either by approving the merger or by imposing conditions different from those recommended by the Competition Commission. Otherwise, the merger is dead.

As with the European Commission, national merger enforcement on occasion takes factors other than competitive impact into account. In the United Kingdom, issues that may be considered include the effect of the proposed merger on employment and on the localities in which the merger partners operate, possible efficiency gains, the degree to which the deal is adequately financed or involves financial overstretch, matters related to national defense, and—in cases involving newspapers—the effect of the consolidation on diversity and plurality of information sources. In Germany, the Federal Cartel Office's decision to prohibit a merger may be overruled if the minister of economics decides that the anticompetitive effects are trumped by the benefits for the economy as a whole or by overriding public interest considerations. A similar regime is in place in France, Spain, and Switzerland.

The introduction of issues unrelated to competitive impact is not the only difference between the U.S. and European antitrust regimes. An important procedural difference also exists. The European authorities go to great efforts to avoid what they consider to be the excesses of the U.S. litigation system. Enforcement agencies, therefore, may proceed far more informally than in the United States. There is often no opportunity to cross-examine hostile presentations, present rebuttal evidence in a formal setting, or determine the timing of proceedings. That puts a premium on informal contacts with enforcement authorities, who are not bound by any of the restrictions against ex parte representations that often inhibit contact between adversaries in U.S. proceedings.

Canadian Antitrust Enforcement

Canadian antitrust law has undergone considerable revision in recent years and now more closely approximates the U.S. regime. The Competition Act prohibits the traditional restrictive practices, and the merger provisions aim to prevent the dilution of competition unless gains in efficiency outweigh the costs of such dilution. The Canadian Competition Bureau has recently published revised draft Intellectual Property Guidelines and a draft Immunity Program and has signed a cooperation agreement with the European Union.

But significant differences between the United States and Canada remain. Unless some recently proposed amendments are eventually enacted, all conspiracy cases are criminal cases under Canadian law. Under Canadian law, price-fixing is not per se unlawful because conspiracies are prohibited only when they restrain or injure competition unduly. Bid-rigging is a per se offense in Canada, but bid-riggers can escape liability by disclosing their agreement.

The penalties for being found guilty of a conspiracy include imprisonment or a fine of up to $10 million (Canadian), or both. While the Competition Act makes no provision for treble damages, plaintiffs may recover their actual losses. Recent enforcement by Canadian authorities against international price-fixing conspiracies has paralleled U.S. enforcement, again with substantial fines being obtained against both corporations and individuals.

The Competition Act, supplemented by merger enforcement guidelines, governs mergers and acquisitions. Canadian merger law makes the attainment of efficiencies that are greater than and offset the effects of any prevention or lessening of competition an absolute defense, even in the case of a merger that demonstrably and substantially lessens competition.

International Merger Notification

As nations around the world enact antitrust laws or add merger notification regimes, businesses find themselves having to notify more and more jurisdictions of their larger deals. Worldwide, some ninety jurisdictions have competition laws; more than sixty of those jurisdictions have merger notification regimes. A transaction involving two European-owned firms, for example, may require notification on six continents, and the approval of the local competition authorities may be a condition to the consummation of the transaction.

Worldwide notification requirements may impose substantial costs and significant delays. The parties to increasingly multinational deals are faced with filing fees for the various notifications, as well as potential legal fees of numerous local counsel. Where transactions are actually investigated by local authorities, substantial compliance costs may result as the authorities request additional information from the parties. Transactions may be delayed for months as a result of waiting periods and investigations, and can impose additional costs on the parties as stock markets react to the delays.

All the more troublesome is the low level of contact required to trigger a notification requirement in many jurisdictions. Most jurisdictions require that some minimum threshold be met, but those thresholds are often quite low. For example, in Brazil a merger involving a firm with more than about $225 million in worldwide turnover will require notification if the target has any local sales.

At this writing, no system to eliminate multiple notification has been devised. Indeed, the European Commission, claiming a lack of sufficient staff and resources to review all the mergers that now come before it, is proposing that some of the smaller transactions be reviewed instead by authorities in the member states. Still, a developing international consensus among antitrust officials points toward a common notification system in the not-too-distant future.

International Antitrust Enforcement Cooperation

Cooperation among antitrust enforcement authorities around the world is clearly on the increase on other fronts as well. No doubt, that results from two facts: frequently, antitrust violators are seen to be multinational companies capable of removing evidence from one jurisdiction to another; and, as various countries' antitrust policies move more closely into alignment, enforcement cooperation makes good policy sense.

Although cooperation agreements are in effect between the United States and Germany (1976), Australia (1982), Canada (1995), the European Union (1991 and 1998), Israel (1999), Japan (1999), Brazil (1999), and Mexico (2000), significant limitations still exist on the ability, certainly of the U.S. government, to make available confidential information protected by specific statutes and grand jury rules. But with the signing into law of the International Antitrust Enforcement Assistance Act of 1994, enforcement cooperation has the potential to move to an entirely new level. The first IAEAA–authorized agreement was signed with Australia in 1999, and the agencies are working toward negotiating others.

The new statute provides the Justice Department and the FTC with the authority to enter into mutual assistance agreements with foreign antitrust authorities that involve the exchange of confidential information.

Foreign antitrust authorities must have laws providing for the preservation of confidentiality equivalent to that required by the laws of the United States, and they must agree to return any information at the conclusion of the investigation or proceeding. Assuming the existence of mutual assistance agreements under the act, the attorney general may request his or her counterpart abroad to issue a search warrant for evidence to be used in the U.S. proceeding. In addition, standard information request procedures allow the raiding of the offices of a German corporation with papers issued by an American court—successfully securing documents for use in an international criminal investigation by the Justice Department. To put it another way, through the use of international cooperation agreements and diplomatic mechanisms, Scotland Yard, the Royal Canadian Mounted Police, and German police become extensions of the FBI and vice versa.

The new statute and the web of enforcement cooperation agreements now being set in place will permit U.S. authorities to defer increasingly to enforcement action by foreign authorities where the conduct takes place outside the United States. The Justice Department recently closed an investigation because the company under investigation had reached an agreement with the European Commission that alleviated any anticompetitive concerns, perhaps the first such example of explicit deference on the record.

Even more strikingly, the Department of Justice recently requested the competitive authorities of the European Commission to investigate anticompetitive conduct by European airlines that seemed to be preventing U.S.–based airline computer reservation systems from competing in Europe. That was the first formal "positive comity" request made under the 1991 U.S.–EU agreement.

Already on the record are several notable instances of successful enforcement cooperation, particularly between the European Union and the United States and between Canada and the United States. In 1994 the Justice Department and the European Commission jointly settled claims against Microsoft, following an investigation characterized by very close cooperation between the two antitrust authorities. Canada and the United States conducted joint criminal prosecutions against defendants in the fax paper and plastic dinnerware markets. Each country drew on its criminal investigative capabilities to ferret out evidence of cartel behavior that would otherwise have been beyond the countries' respective jurisdictions. Similar cooperation has occurred between the U.S. and UK authorities in connection with a telecommunications joint venture and also between the enforcement agencies in the United States and Germany in connection with an acquisition in the automobile transmission industry.

Those are only a few examples of the cooperation that occurs, and, as enforcement officials often point out, much more cooperation and consultation occur on an informal level and go unreported as telephone calls are traded almost daily between European and U.S. antitrust enforcers. As more such agreements are put into place, more joint investigations will occur, and simultaneous dual prosecutions in different countries will very likely become the order of the day. But heated international disputes among competition authorities will nevertheless continue to occur, especially in the case of mergers that have major efficiency advantages in one country but are seen as disadvantaging competitors in another, and in instances in which different authorities disagree on economic issues, such as the definition of *predation* and the possibility of anticompetitive bundling.

Other disputes will inevitably arise when legislatures or antitrust enforcement officials or both in one country come to believe that officials in another country are acting not to protect competition, but to preserve some perceived national interest. Perhaps the most publicized instance of such conflict occurred when the European Commission seemed likely to bar the 1997 merger of Boeing and McDonnell-Douglas. U.S. lawmakers questioned the Europeans' authority to challenge the merger and suggested that competition concerns had taken a back seat to the promotion of Airbus. A trade war loomed and was averted only when Boeing agreed to modify the transaction in a way acceptable to the European Commission.

The most recent transatlantic controversy grew out of GE's attempt to acquire Honeywell. The Department of Justice approved the transaction with ease, but the authorities in Brussels concluded that after the merger GE would be able to use its dominant position to overwhelm its competitors. The gap between the two enforcement authorities was significant—but both agencies were at pains to explain how rare such interagency disagreement actually was.

Those disagreements will not be limited to specific cases. Authorities in different countries disagree as to whether the World Trade Organization should become involved in antitrust matters, and all remain slightly nervous at the extraterritorial reach of the laws in other countries. Nevertheless, the trend toward international cooperation in antitrust enforcement, driven as it is by the increasingly international reach of most of the world's major corporations, is likely to continue.

THIRTEEN

Compliance

The old maxim that an ounce of prevention is worth a pound of cure carries extra authority in the field of antitrust. Where jail terms, hundred-million-dollar recoveries, and enormous litigation expenses can follow hard upon a corporate misstep, businesses prefer the monotony of never being a defendant in antitrust litigation. In fact, because of that self-interest, the American business community and its lawyers are themselves in the front line of antitrust enforcement. An ounce of antitrust compliance effort today is worth pounds of litigation cure in the future.

So how to organize a compliance program? The most important element is management support. Unless enthusiasm for the compliance program comes from the top, it will be ineffective with employees. The first step is clear leadership endorsement of antitrust compliance and firm imposition of responsibility—and accountability—on the shoulders of individual supervisors for ensuring that their employees not only participate in the program but take the lessons to heart.

An efficient and effective compliance program will have to involve an antitrust lawyer. That lawyer should be asked to put together a program that includes the issuance of written guidelines, an antitrust presentation to important officials, a review of document procedures, and periodic antitrust audits.

For the entire program to be credible, it must be useful day in and day out to the people who will hear it. Such programs are not fungible. Tailoring the compliance program to each company is essential, because the program must take into account the needs, history, and special ways of doing business unique both to an industry and to a company.

First of all, the antitrust lawyer must have access to essential facts about the company and about the industry through the study of business files and interviews of senior supervisors. He will then analyze the facts. He must anticipate so that he will be prepared to advise. He must think aggressively, debunk myths, and quarrel with received wisdom. No two compliance programs are ever the same. But each must get across a minimum amount of relatively complicated information in a way that is user-friendly.

Written Guidelines

A written policy statement, accompanied by a simplified primer (such as this book) that can be kept at the employee's desk, gives the compliance program a permanence that one-time oral exposition cannot claim. The written policy statement should require the employee, as a matter of company obligation, to read and become familiar with the contents of the antitrust primer. Perhaps an acknowledgment of receipt and understanding should be required annually from each recipient. It would also be well to include in a prominent place the language of Section 14 of the Clayton

Act that imposes criminal liability on all officers or directors who authorize or participate in any of the company's antitrust violations. In that way the lesson and the incentive to learn it are strengthened.

Compliance Sessions

Once the written material is prepared and distributed, it is time to drive the message home. That is an important part of demonstrating a company's commitment to the project: a senior official of the company should open the meeting by endorsing the program and introducing the team—lawyers and business people— who will run the meeting and answer questions.

Why both lawyers and business people? It is a fact of life that lawyers, whether in-house counsel or antitrust lawyers from large firms, are too easily dismissed as irrelevant. Visible endorsement by the management is required at that critical point. In addition, the substance of the presentation will be richer, its persuasive impact greater, if joint teams are used.

The senior antitrust lawyer should personally make the presentation. Large law firms, in particular, sometimes have a tendency to delegate that task to a younger lawyer who is still learning his job. That is not good enough. The material is difficult, sometimes confusing. Its effective communication requires a memorable performance.

The mode of presentation is critical. Emphasis on the practical over the theoretical is essential. Elaborate explanations of legal minutiae are ineffective. Lawyers must not be content simply to list prohibitions but must be prepared to give answers that company personnel can live with and that will not seem at odds with the necessity of doing business in a tough competitive world.

That initial session is a general review, but it can, if necessary, be followed by later, smaller sessions that deal in greater depth with special problem areas, which may more directly implicate the responsibilities of specialized employees and supervisors.

Whatever the plan, those sessions should be a continual feature of the company's regimen. Like fire drills, antitrust compliance sessions produce benefit through repetition. Unless the subject is kept alive in everyone's mind, it will gradually recede in importance and too soon become an inconvenience or irrelevancy.

Documents

At the same time that the compliance sessions cover substantive antitrust law, they should probably also cover documents and internal document procedures. Documents are of particular concern in antitrust cases. There are three problems: first, to ensure that the documents, if they must be created, are accurate, conservatively stated, and devoid of overheated competitive threats or overstated competitive boasts, both of which can come back to haunt the company later on; second, to ensure that a system is in place so that troublesome or ambiguous conduct is supported by documentation showing justification and establishing the foundation for sound legal defenses should the need later arise; and third, to ensure that a records retention system exists that serves to rid the company of ancient files—including computer files—with no current use, thereby avoiding misuse of certain documents against the company in later antitrust litigation.

The creation of new documents should be governed by antitrust sensitivity as to how they will look if ever introduced in evidence against the company. The author of the casual e-mail must be as alert to antitrust risks as the corporate secretary reviewing board of director minutes. Sloppy drafting, unnecessarily warlike phrasing, and allusions to "obliteration," "incineration," or "wiping out the competition" are unnecessary. Words such as *agreed* are antitrust dynamite that may explode at a later date and should be confined to those situations in which they are precisely correct. Documents that are tagged with legends such as "Destroy after reading" are worth their weight in gold to plaintiffs. Any time a mistake is found in a document that will nevertheless be on file, a corrective memorandum should be immediately inserted into the files. Always remember that the fact finder evaluating those documents as evidence in antitrust litigation many years later is likely to be tempted to place the most sinister construction on the language.

As to explanatory documents in the files, many business people wonder why it makes sense to be creating evidence in that way. But as we have seen, antitrust trials can focus on the defendant's motivation or on whether or not sufficient business justification exists for challenged conduct. The plaintiff will argue that such justifications are the latter-day inventions of imaginative defense counsel and that instead the conduct was originally undertaken for the purpose of squashing some upstart competitor. How much easier it will be to establish the truth of the defense if at the time of the conduct simple steps are taken to document the business context and the specific reasons that the conduct seemed justifiable and reasonable. A contemporary document of that kind speaks far louder than the testimony many years later of company witnesses, whose views will be subject to the interpretation that they are engaged in after-the-fact rationalization.

Finally, every company should have a document retention program. What is required is a system for destroying those documents that are no longer of any use in a company's business. Obviously, the purpose of that policy is to minimize filing costs; in the event of litigation, to minimize the cost of the document search; and, most important, to decrease sharply the possibility that the documents will be used against the company in some later litigation.

The program should apply to all files of the corporation, including personal files. The executives should be told that their papers kept at home or in their automobiles are subject to subpoena. Diary entries, telephone logs, and expense account vouchers are all grist for the grand jury. As dramatically illustrated in the Iran-Contra investigation, computer files and backup systems have increasingly been used to resurrect documents, the hard copies of which were destroyed. So that the files do not remain in the computer memory in perpetuity, special document retention procedures have to be focused on those files.

It is important that the document retention program be consistently implemented because, in the event of an investigation, counsel will be called upon to explain to skeptical government prosecutors the operation of the program in detail and any inconsistencies in its implementation. An otherwise perfect document retention program can be converted in a prosecutor's mind into a conspiracy to destroy evidence when there seems to be selectivity in the missing documents.

Obviously—and this is essential—once an investigation is undertaken or a lawsuit filed, it is unlawful and indeed suicidal for a company to begin to destroy relevant documents. Procedures therefore have to be built into the document retention program so that once litigation or investigations have been instituted, the destruction program is suspended as to all conceivably relevant documents.

Periodic Audits

Finally, it is wise for a business to institute periodic antitrust audits. Much like physical examinations, those audits are periodic efforts by businesses to confirm their antitrust health. Because of problems of privilege, those audits should be conducted by lawyers. Their function is to ascertain that the antitrust compliance program is actually working and to remedy any lax implementation or defective understanding before it can cause major difficulties for a business that is trying to do its best.

Pricing, sales, planning, and market research offices and files ought to be the focus, but others should not be neglected. The lawyer who is performing the audit should report the findings in detail to the company's general counsel, who must then make decisions on the need for an antitrust update or specialized compliance seminars to deal with newly appearing problems and must also remedy all problems that were discovered during the audit.

If there seem to be concerns that crop up on a steady basis, the business might consider establishing a "safe harbor" procedure. Such a procedure is based on the principle that every employee in the company must feel free to give information to and seek advice from some trusted company employee without fear of reprisal or condemnation. Indeed, as part of a compliance program, it must be clear to all that any suspicious activity, any nagging questions, or even idle curiosity or "hypothetical situations" should be brought directly to the general counsel's office, without having to go through the chain of command or to notify a supervisor. Despite its slightly subversive sound, that kind of practice benefits the company, since antitrust problems, even if they involve a supervisor, are much more likely to be exposed.

Although all of that may appear quite complicated, antitrust concerns are now a fact of life in American business. Many companies already have rather intricate compliance programs. Many caught in the antitrust vise for the first time quickly institute them. They can be as simple as necessary or as complicated and sophisticated as appropriate. They can be instituted easily and with modest expenditure, but one thing is certain—they may save some business executives years of their lives.

FOURTEEN

Some Common-Sense Guidelines

As the previous chapters demonstrate, the antitrust laws combine a few black-and-white proscriptions with many grayer directives that depend on the facts of each case. Offering businesses the assurance of a list of "dos and don'ts" is therefore difficult, not to mention risky, in this era of easily provoked malpractice actions. Nevertheless, counting on the intelligence of our readers and the availability to them of counsel, we offer a few guidelines.

- *Do not discuss prices with your competitors.* That is one of those black-and-white areas. The enforcement authorities can be counted on to bring a criminal prosecution if they learn that you have met with your competitors to fix prices or any other terms of sale. Jail time is increasingly common.
- *Do not agree with your competitor to stay out of each other's markets.* It may be tempting to seek freedom of action in one part of the country by agreeing with a competitor not to go west if he will not come east. Avoid that temptation. The conse-

145

quences of the discovery of such behavior by the enforcement authorities are likely to be the same as the unearthing of a price-fixing conspiracy.

- *Feel free to join trade associations and to participate in activities that do not affect the vigor of your competition with your fellow members.* Safety standards, industry-sponsored promotion of a generic product ("take the family to the movies"; "wool is comfortable in the summer"; "natural gas burns cleaner"), and other activities that do not diminish the intensity of your competition with others in the industry are perfectly acceptable. So, too, are exchanges of information that do not affect prices in future transactions. But beware of meetings with competitors that result in discussions of business tactics, customers, costs, and ultimately prices. Be on guard at all times at trade association functions; leave if the meeting turns to what might be construed as price-fixing or market sharing.

- *Do not join forces with some of your competitors to the disadvantage of a few others.* Here we enter a gray area. Some forms of cooperation, such as joint research and development activities, are permissible if their main purpose is to improve efficiency; others, especially those that deny the excluded competitor access to an essential facility on reasonable terms, are more questionable.

- *Compete vigorously for all the business you can get.* There is nothing in the antitrust laws that penalizes success achieved by lawful methods. Adopt any new marketing or pricing strategies for which you have a sound business justification. If you are efficient enough to offer a product that garners a large market share on its merits—because it is either cheaper or better, or both—do not worry. Big is not bad.

- *Do not price below some meaningful measure of cost with the intention of using deep pockets to drive out a competitor or discourage a new entrant.* That is one of those gray areas, since some below-cost pricing is acceptable (for example, introductory offers) and since the courts have not clearly defined the measure of cost to be used. But that is an area of sufficient exposure to warrant careful review of any planned actions, particularly if you have a large market share.

- *If you have some significant market power, consider the effect on competitors of any planned action.* Market power can be measured either by your share of the market—and most business people do not need an elaborate economic study to define the product and geographic dimensions of the market in which they are operating—or by the possession of considerable freedom of action in setting prices. If the planned action is likely to hurt your competitors badly, be sure that such harm is a byproduct of moves that have a sound business justification.

- *Feel free to suggest retail prices to dealers but not to coerce them to accept those prices.* Send them suggested price lists and promotional literature mentioning price. But do not extract an agreement from them to charge that price or threaten cancellation of dealerships if they elect an independent pricing strategy: guidance, yes; persuasion, yes; agreements, no; coercion, no.

- *Impose such restrictions on distributors and dealers as contribute to your ability to compete with rival brands.*

You can cancel nonperforming dealers, but keep good records to document their poor performance in case a dispute arises about the circumstances.

- *Do not tie the sale of one product to another.* Such arrangements might be allowed in a few rare instances—to ensure effective functioning of complicated equipment, to name one. But they generally fall afoul of the law.
- *Use exclusive dealing arrangements if they are justified by business necessity.* The higher your market share and the longer the term of the agreement, the more important a compelling business justification.
- *Charge all customers the same price, unless the cost of serving them varies.* But feel free to cut prices to any customer to meet the lower price of a competitor.
- *Institute and support a vigorous, custom-designed antitrust compliance program.* Only a commitment by very top management, supported by competent counsel, can provide the ounce of prevention that prevents the authorities and private plaintiffs from administering their weighty cures: jail terms, fines, and large damage claims.
- *Consult with counsel when specific problems or questionable activities occur.* While this book gives you a general overview of the law and the issues, antitrust law is highly fact-specific. There is no substitute for competent advice based on the detailed facts unique to your situation.

FIFTEEN

Epilogue

We hope that this brief review of the antitrust laws will make them more comprehensible to the nonlawyer. We also hope that it will show that the statutes and the court decisions flowing from them are sufficiently consistent to provide a reasonable guide to business behavior.

We hope, too, that greater familiarity with the antitrust laws will make clear their key role in America's astounding economic development. The preservation of competition has been an essential ingredient in the development of a technologically advanced, high-income, consumer-driven economy that remains the envy of the world.

It was not always thus. When America was suffering through the Great Depression in the 1930s, the Soviet model of centralized direction of economic affairs became fashionable. After World War II, critics of the competitive system, unhappy with its allocative results, looked to the socialist societies of Britain and Sweden for guides to superior economic performance, or to France's "indicative planning."

Meanwhile, America's economy ground on, producing enormous wealth and distributing it widely, as firms vied with each other to keep costs and prices down and to discover new products that might appeal to consumers. Some industries, of course, managed to avoid tough competition, at least for a while. Firms in America's auto and steel industries became so beguiled by their market shares that they grew inattentive to costs and to the need to innovate. Enter foreign firms—hungrier and leaner—to offer consumers alternatives that the sleepier domestic firms had not bothered to explore.

Significantly, America's smaller, more competitive companies continued to thrive and to provide the engine for an enormous growth in jobs. Those firms' ability to enter markets and compete with established firms is guaranteed by the antitrust laws. Once established, many undoubtedly would have preferred the easier life of the cartelist, but the antitrust laws, enforced by government officials and private parties, deprived them of the opportunity to fix prices or merge their way to market dominance.

It would be foolish to claim that America's economic success is attributable solely to the antitrust laws. But it would be equally foolish to ignore the effect of those laws, not only in the narrow sense of preserving competition but in the more fundamental sense of creating a society in which innovation is prized rather than feared, and in which government is obliged to encourage entrepreneurship and new entry, rather than to protect existing firms from competition. The generators of the 1990s' wave of creative destruction did not choose Silicon Valley over the Ruhr Valley by chance;

they did so because they knew that American institutions and law favor the newcomer.

That seems to surprise those who contend that the antitrust laws—more than 100 years old—are something of an anachronism, perhaps appropriate to the era of big steel and big oil, but a hindrance to economic development in an increasingly globalized economy that depends as much on human brainpower as on physical assets. Those people question whether laws drafted to cope with problems in early and midtwentieth–century competition can sensibly be applied to today's international, high-tech, "knowledge" companies.

Fortunately, it has been possible to adapt the antitrust laws to new circumstances, while remaining true to their fundamental procompetition principles. Amendments clarifying the permissible scope of joint ventures in research and development and in overseas markets, guidelines relating to specific industries such as health care, and other guidelines to lawful conduct for firms producing and using intellectual property have all been enacted or promulgated as part of a continuing process of modernizing the application of antitrust laws, one of which has passed its 110th birthday. But the basic ban on collusive activities and monopolizing behavior remains.

America's procompetition policies have survived, once again, despite the apparent attractiveness of other models. Japan's highly cartelized economy for a while seemed so successful that America's continued reliance on competition was called into question. But, even before the Japanese economy lapsed into severe recession, it became obvious that Japan's cartels keep prices to consumers at levels that can only be described as extortionate and depress living standards to an extent that would be unacceptable in the United States. Meanwhile, the German model of interrelated financial and industrial firms, working closely with their government, lost its temporary appeal when it became apparent that many once-efficient German firms had failed to innovate sufficiently to keep pace with Germany's international rivals and that German industry is now so burdened with social costs as to be noncompetitive in many markets.

For those and other reasons, the Japanese and German models, like the centrally directed economies of an earlier era, hardly seem credible alternatives to a competitive economy such as ours.

American industry certainly faces many problems. But an excess of competition should not be included on the roster of villains. Small competitive firms continue to grow and prosper; large industrial behemoths that rest on the laurels of historical market share continue to shrivel. Firms that must be lean and mean to meet domestic competition are and will remain America's best representatives in the international arena. And antitrust law's insistence on competition, a policy now increasingly gaining force abroad, is the best guarantor of a growing and efficient world economy.

Appendix A

Basic Antitrust Statutes

The Sherman Act, 1890

Sec. 1. (amended) Every contract, combination in the form of trust or otherwise, or conspiracy, in restraint of trade or commerce among the several States, or with foreign nations, is hereby declared to be illegal. Every person who shall make any contract or engage in any combination or conspiracy hereby declared to be illegal shall be deemed guilty of a felony, and, on conviction thereof, shall be punished by fine not exceeding $10,000,000 if a corporation, or, if any other person, $350,000, or by imprisonment not exceeding three years, or by both said punishments, in the discretion of the court. [15 U.S.C. § 1]

Sec. 2. Every person who shall monopolize, or attempt to monopolize, or combine or conspire with any other person or persons, to monopolize any part of the trade or commerce among the several States, or with foreign nations, shall be deemed guilty of a felony, and, on conviction thereof, shall be punished by fine not exceeding $10,000,000 if a corporation, or, if any other person, $350,000, or by imprisonment not

153

exceeding three years, or by both said punishments, in the discretion of the court. [15 U.S.C. § 2]

The Clayton Act, 1914

Sec. 2. (amended) (a) It shall be unlawful for any person engaged in commerce, in the course of such commerce, either directly or indirectly, to discriminate in price between different purchasers of commodities of like grade and quality, where either or any of the purchases involved in such discrimination are in commerce, where such commodities are sold for use, consumption, or resale within the United States or any Territory thereof or the District of Columbia or any insular possession or other place under the jurisdiction of the United States, and where the effect of such discrimination may be substantially to lessen competition or tend to create a monopoly in any line of commerce, or to injure, destroy, or prevent competition with any person who either grants or knowingly receives the benefit of such discrimination, or with customers of either of them: *Provided,* That nothing herein contained shall prevent differentials which make only due allowance for differences in the cost of manufacture, sale, or delivery resulting from the differing methods or quantities in which such commodities are to such purchasers sold or delivered: *Provided, however,* That the Federal Trade Commission may, after due investigation and hearing to all interested parties, fix and establish quantity limits, and revise the same as it finds necessary, as to particular commodities or classes of commodities, where it finds that available purchasers in greater quantities are so few as to render differentials on account thereof unjustly discriminatory or promotive of monopoly in any line of commerce; and the foregoing shall then not be construed to permit differentials based on differences in quantities greater than those so fixed and established: *And provided further,* That nothing herein contained shall prevent persons engaged in selling goods, wares, or merchandise in commerce from selecting their own customers in bona fide transactions and not in restraint of trade: *And provided further,* That nothing herein contained shall prevent price changes from time to time where in response to changing conditions affecting the market for or the marketability of the goods concerned, such as but not limited to actual or imminent deterioration of perishable goods, obsolescence of seasonal goods, distress sales under court process, or sales in good faith in discontinuance of business in the goods concerned. [15 U.S.C. § 13(a)]

(b) Upon proof being made, at any hearing on a complaint under this section, that there has been discrimination in price or services or facilities furnished, the burden of rebutting the prima-facie case thus made by showing justification shall be upon the person charged with a violation of this section, and unless justification shall be affirmatively shown, the Commission is authorized to issue an order terminating the discrimination: *Provided, however,* That nothing herein contained shall prevent a seller rebutting the prima-facie case thus made by showing that his lower price or the furnishing of services of facilities to any purchaser or purchasers was made in good faith to meet an equally low price of a competitor, or the services or facilities furnished by a competitor. [15 U.S.C. § 13(b)]

(c) It shall be unlawful for any person engaged in commerce, in the course of such commerce, to pay or grant, or to receive or accept, anything of value as a commission, brokerage, or other compensation, or any allowance or discount in lieu thereof, except for services rendered in connection with the sale or purchase of goods, wares, or merchandise, either to the other party to such transaction or to an agent, representative, or other intermediary therein where such intermediary is acting in fact for or in behalf, or is subject to the direct or indirect control, of any party to such transaction other than the person by whom such compensation is so granted or paid. [15 U.S.C. § 13(c)]

(d) It shall be unlawful for any person engaged in commerce to pay or contract for the payment of anything of value to or for the benefit of a customer of such person in the course of such commerce as compensation or in consideration for any services or facilities furnished by or through such customer in connection with the processing, handling, sale, or offering for sale of any products or commodities manufactured, sold, or offered for sale by such person, unless such payment or consideration is available on proportionally equal terms to all other customers competing in the distribution of such products or commodities. [15 U.S.C. § 13(d)]

(e) It shall be unlawful for any person to discriminate in favor of one purchaser against another purchaser or purchasers of a commodity bought for resale, with or without processing, by contracting to furnish or furnishing, or by contributing to the furnishing of, any services or facilities connected with the processing, handling, sale, or offering for sale of such commodity so purchased upon terms not accorded to all purchasers on proportionally equal terms. [15 U.S.C. § 13(e)]

(f) It shall be unlawful for any person engaged in commerce, in the course of such commerce, knowingly to induce or receive a discrimination in price which is prohibited by this section. [15 U.S.C. § 13(f)]

Sec. 3. It shall be unlawful for any person engaged in commerce, in the course of such commerce, to lease or make a sale or contract for sale of goods, wares, merchandise, machinery, supplies, or other commodities, whether patented or unpatented, for use, consumption, or resale within the United States or any Territory thereof or the District of Columbia or any insular possession or other place under the jurisdiction of the United States, or fix a price charged therefor, or discount from, or rebate upon, such price, on the condition, agreement, or understanding that the lessee or purchaser thereof shall not use or deal in the goods, wares, merchandise, machinery, supplies, or other commodities of a competitor or competitors of the lessor or seller, where the effect of such lease, sale, or contract for sale or such condition, agreement, or understanding may be to substantially lessen competition or tend to create a monopoly in any line of commerce. [15 U.S.C. § 14]

Sec. 7. No person engaged in commerce or in any activity affecting commerce shall acquire, directly or indirectly, the whole or any part of the stock or other share capital and no person subject to the jurisdiction of the Federal Trade Commission shall acquire the whole or any part of the assets of another person engaged also in commerce or in any activity affecting commerce, where in any line of commerce or in any activity affecting commerce in any section of the country, the effect of such acquisition may be substantially to lessen competition, or to tend to create a monopoly. [15 U.S.C. § 18]

The Federal Trade Commission Act, 1914

Sec. 5. (a)(1) Unfair methods of competition in or affecting commerce, and unfair or deceptive acts or practices in or affecting commerce, are hereby declared unlawful. [15 U.S.C. § 45(a)(1)]

Appendix B
The Herfindahl-Hirschman Index

The Herfindahl-Hirschman index (HHI) was designed as an aid in evaluating market concentration. Before performing the HHI calculation, first determine what the relevant market is, who the market participants are, and what the market share of each participant is. Next, calculate market shares by using dollar sales, unit sales, or physical capacity, depending upon which is the best indicator of a firm's future competitive significance. Typically, annual data are used unless they are unrepresentative in a particular market. Furthermore, sales or capacity that is unavailable to respond to an increase in price in the market is not included in the measurement of a firm's market share.

The HHI is then calculated by summing the squares of the individual market shares of all market participants. By summing the squares, the HHI gives proportionately greater weight to the market shares of larger firms; the higher the HHI, the greater the market concentration. A market consisting of four firms with market shares of 25 percent, for example, will have an HHI of $(25^2 + 25^2 + 25^2 + 25^2)$, or 2,500. In contrast, if a market consists of four firms, two firms with a 40 percent share of the market and two firms with a 10 percent share of the market, the HHI will be $(40^2 + 40^2 + 10^2 + 10^2)$, or 3,400. The second market has a higher HHI because the higher market shares of the two larger firms were squared. Although both markets are highly concentrated by the current standards of the enforcement agencies, the second market is more highly concentrated and more prone to collusion. HHI analysis is not meant to substitute for the substantive economic evaluation of a merger. Rather, it is simply a tool designed to aid in the analysis.

The Department of Justice and the Federal Trade Commission Horizontal Merger Guidelines use HHI calculations to classify market concentration. A postmerger HHI above 1,800 suggests a highly concentrated market. A postmerger HHI between 1,000 and 1,800 suggests a moderately concentrated market, and a postmerger HHI below 1,000 suggests an unconcentrated market. The greater the concentration in the industry, the more likely the merger will result in antitrust scrutiny. Those thresholds serve merely as proxies for market concentration; there will likely be no difference in treatment between a market with an HHI of 1,805 and one with an HHI of 1,795.

Appendix C
The EC Treaty

Art. 81 (1) The following shall be prohibited as incompatible with the common market: all agreements between undertakings, decisions by associations of undertakings and concerted practices which may affect trade between Member States and which have as their object or effect the prevention, restriction or distortion of competition within the common market, and in particular those which: (a) directly or indirectly fix purchase or selling prices or any other trading conditions; (b) limit or control production, markets, technical development, or investment; (c) share markets or sources of supply; (d) apply dissimilar conditions to equivalent transactions with other trading parties, thereby placing them at a competitive disadvantage; (e) make the conclusion of contracts subject to acceptance by the other parties of supplementary obligations which, by their nature or according to commercial usage, have no connection with the subject of such contracts.

(2) Any agreements or decisions prohibited pursuant to this Article shall be automatically void.

(3) The provisions of paragraph 1 may, however, be declared inapplicable in the case of: (a) any agreement or category of agreements between undertakings; (b) any decision or category of decisions by associations of undertakings; (c) any concerted practice or category of concerted practices which contributes to improving the production or distribution of goods or to promoting technical or economic progress while allowing consumers a fair share of the resulting benefit, and which does not: (i) impose on the undertakings concerned restrictions which are not indispensable to the attainment of these objectives; (ii) afford such undertakings the possibility of eliminating competition in respect of a substantial part of the products in question.

Art. 82. Any abuse by one or more undertakings of a dominant position within the common market or in a substantial part of it shall be prohibited as incompatible with the common market insofar as it may affect trade between Member States. Such abuse may, in particular, consist in: (a) directly or indirectly imposing unfair purchase or selling prices or other unfair trading conditions; (b) limiting production, markets or technical development to the prejudice of consumers; (c) applying dissimilar conditions to equivalent transactions with other trading parties, thereby placing them at a competitive disadvantage; (d) making the conclusion of contracts subject to acceptance by the other parties of supplementary obligations which, by their nature or according to commercial usage, have no connection with the subject of such contracts.

Appendix D
Further Reading

It is difficult to select from the voluminous literature on antitrust policy a few works that might be worth the while of a nonspecialist interested in learning more, but not much more, about the subject. Our highly idiosyncratic suggestions follow.

The history of the antitrust laws, and especially of what was going on in the minds of their congressional sponsors, is set forth in a well-written volume by Hans B. Thorelli *(The Federal Antitrust Policy: Origination of an American Tradition)*, now available from University Microfilms International (Ann Arbor, Michigan: Out-of-Print Books, 1992). The case that the antitrust laws have a social as well as an economic goal is best made by Joel B. Dirlam and Alfred E. Kahn in their *Fair Competition: The Law and Economics of Antitrust Policy* (Westport, Connecticut: Greenwood Press, 1970). The contrary position, that antitrust is about maximizing consumer welfare, and nothing more, is powerfully argued by Judge Robert H. Bork in his *Antitrust Paradox: A Policy at War with Itself* (New York: Free Press, 1993).

The best annual update of developments in antitrust law is Phillip E. Areeda and Herbert Hovenkamp's annual supplement, *Antitrust Law: An Analysis of Antitrust Principles and Their Application,* now published by Aspen Law and Business (Gaithersburg, Maryland). Valuable guidance for businessmen engaged in mergers is provided in Caswell Hobbs and Robert Schlossberg's *Antitrust Strategies for Mergers, Acquisitions, Joint Ventures, and Strategic Alliances* (Washington, D.C.: Lexis Publishing, 2000). A good, if bulky and technical, compendium of the current thinking of economists on a variety of antitrust issues can be found in the *Handbook of Industrial Organization,* edited by Richard Schmalensee and Robert Willig (New York: North Holland, 1989). And a useful text is *Industrial Organization Economics: Theory and Evidence* by Donald A. Hay and Derek J. Morris (New York: Oxford University Press, 1991). The latter author is the chairman of Britain's Competition Commission.

Notes

In an effort to make the text itself readable, we have omitted many case references and citations. For those interested in exploring specific rules and fact situations further, we include some of those omitted references here.

Page 1

United States v. Topco Associates, Inc., 405 U.S. 596 (1972).

Page 12

Appalachian Coals, Inc. v. United States, 288 U.S. 344 (1933).

Page 16

Copperweld Corp. v. Independence Tube Corp., 467 U.S. 752 (1984).

Summit Health, Ltd. v. Pinhas, 111 S. Ct. 1842 (1991).

Standard Oil Co. v. United States, 221 U.S. 1 (1911).

Page 17

Northern Pacific Railway v. United States, 356 U.S. 1 (1958).

United States v. Trenton Potteries Co., 273 U.S. 392 (1927).

United States v. Topco Associates, Inc., 405 U.S. 596 (1972).

Page 18

Northwest Wholesale Stationers v. Pacific Stationery & Printing Co., 472 U.S. 284 (1985).

National Society of Professional Engineers v. United States, 435 U.S. 679 (1978).

Page 19

Northern Pacific Railway v. United States, 356 U.S. 1 (1958).

Page 20

Apex Hosiery Co. v. Leader, 310 U.S. 469 (1940).

Page 22

Federal Trade Commission v. Sperry & Hutchinson Co., 405 U.S. 233 (1972).

Page 23

Boise Cascade Corp. v. Federal Trade Commission, 637 F.2d 573 (9th Cir. 1980).

Page 30

United States v. E. I. duPont de Nemours & Co., 351 U.S. 377 (1956).

Page 31

Brown Shoe Co. v. United States, 370 U.S. 294 (1962).

Page 33

Federal Trade Commission v. Indiana Federation of Dentists, 476 U.S. 447 (1986).

Northwest Wholesale Stationers, Inc. v. Pacific Stationery & Printing Co., 472 U.S. 284 (1985).

Page 34

United States v. General Dynamics Corp., 415 U.S. 486 (1974).

United States v. Baker Hughes, Inc., 908 F.2d 981 (D.C. Cir. 1990).

Eastman Kodak Co. v. Image Technical Services, 504 U.S. 451 (1992).

Page 35

United States v. E. I. duPont de Nemours & Co., 351 U.S. 377 (1956).

Page 36

Oahu Gas Service, Inc. v. Pacific Resources, Inc., 838 F.2d 360 (9th Cir. 1988).

Page 37

United States v. Grinnell Corp., 384 U.S. 563 (1966).

United States v. Aluminum Co. of America, 148 F.2d 416 (2d Cir. 1945).

Page 38

American Tobacco Co. v. United States, 328 U.S. 781 (1946).

Page 39

Times-Picayune Publishing Co. v. United States, 345 U.S. 594 (1953).

Page 40

Cargill, Inc. v. Monfort of Colorado, Inc., 479 U.S. 104 (1986).

Neumann v. Reinforced Earth Co., 786 F.2d 424 (D.C. Cir. 1986).

MCI Communications Corp. v. American Telephone & Telegraph Co., 708 F.2d 1081 (7th Cir. 1983).

Berkey Photo, Inc. v. Eastman Kodak Co., 603 F.2d 263 (2d Cir. 1979).

Page 41

United States v. Grinnell Corp., 384 U.S. 563 (1966).

Aspen Skiing Co. v. Aspen Highlands Skiing Corp., 472 U.S. 585 (1985).

Page 42

Berkey Photo, Inc. v. Eastman Kodak Co., 603 F.2d 263 (2d Cir. 1979).

Aspen Skiing Co. v. Aspen Highlands Skiing Corp., 472 U.S. 585 (1985).

United States v. Microsoft Corp., 1995-2 Trade Cases (CCH) ¶ 71,096 (D.D.C. 1995).

Page 43

United States v. Microsoft Corp., 2001-1 Trade Cases (CCH) ¶ 73,321 (D.C. Cir. 2001).

Page 44

United States v. Socony-Vacuum Oil Co., 310 U.S. 150 (1940).

Page 45

United States v. Socony-Vacuum Oil Co., 310 U.S. 150 (1940).

Page 46

Catalano, Inc. v. Target Sales, Inc., 446 U.S. 643 (1980).

United States v. American Radiator & Standard Sanitary Corp., 433 F.2d 174 (3d Cir. 1970).

Federal Trade Commission v. Cement Institute, 333 U.S. 683 (1948).

Plymouth Dealers' Association v. United States, 279 F.2d 128 (9th Cir. 1960).

Goldfarb v. Virginia State Bar, 421 U.S. 773 (1975).

Page 47

Arizona v. Maricopa County Medical Society, 457 U.S. 332 (1982).

Broadcast Music, Inc. v. Columbia Broadcasting System, Inc., 441 U.S. 1 (1979).

Page 48

National Collegiate Athletic Association v. Board of Regents of the University of Oklahoma, 468 U.S. 85 (1984).

Page 49

National Society of Professional Engineers v. United States, 435 U.S. 679 (1978).

Barnett Pontiac-Datsun v. Federal Trade Commission, 955 F.2d 457 (6th Cir. 1992).

Maple Flooring Manufacturers Association v. United States, 268 U.S. 563 (1925).

United States v. Container Corp. of America, 393 U.S. 333 (1969).

Page 50

Quality Trailer Products Corp., 5 Trade Reg. Rep. (CCH) (FTC August 11, 1992).

Page 51

United States v. Topco Associates, Inc., 405 U.S. 596 (1972).

Palmer v. BRG of Georgia, Inc., 111 S. Ct. 401 (1990).

Lektro-Vend Corp. v. Vendo Co., 660 F.2d 255 (7th Cir. 1981).

Addyston Pipe & Steel Co. v. United States, 175 U.S. 211 (1899).

Page 52

Radiant Burners, Inc. v. Peoples Gas Light & Coke Co., 364 U.S. 656 (1961).

Associated Press v. United States, 326 U.S. 1 (1944).

Klor's, Inc. v. Broadway-Hale Stores, Inc., 359 U.S. 207 (1959).

Page 53

Northwest Wholesale Stationers, Inc. v. Pacific Stationery & Printing Co., 472 U.S. 284 (1985).

Page 54

National Collegiate Athletic Association v. Board of Regents of the University of Oklahoma, 468 U.S. 85 (1984).

Broadcast Music, Inc. v. Columbia Broadcasting System, Inc., 441 U.S. 1 (1979).

Brunswick Corp., 94 F.T.C. 1174 (1979).

Page 65

Brown Shoe Co. v. United States, 370 U.S. 294 (1962).

United States v. Von's Grocery Co., 384 U.S. 270 (1966).

Page 66

Brown Shoe Co. v. United States, 370 U.S. 294 (1962).

United States v. General Dynamics Corp., 415 U.S. 486 (1974).

Page 67

United States v. Baker Hughes, Inc., 908 F.2d 981 (D.C. Cir. 1990).

Federal Trade Commission v. Elders Grain, Inc., 868 F.2d 901 (7th Cir. 1989).

Page 73

Dr. Miles Medical Co. v. John D. Park & Sons Co., 220 U.S. 373 (1911).

United States v. Colgate & Co., 250 U.S. 300 (1919).

Page 74

Business Electronics Corp. v. Sharp Electronics Corp., 485 U.S. 717 (1988).

Monsanto Co. v. Spray-Rite Service Corp., 465 U.S. 752 (1984).

State Oil Co. v. Khan, 118 S. Ct. 275 (1997).

Page 75

Isaksen v. Vermont Castings, Inc., 825 F.2d 1158 (7th Cir. 1987).

Newberry v. Washington Post Co., 438 F. Supp. 470 (D.D.C. 1977).

Simpson v. Union Oil Co., 377 U.S. 13 (1964).

Santa Clara Valley Distribution Co. v. Pabst Brewing Co., 556 F.2d 942 (9th Cir. 1977).

Hanson v. Shell Oil Co., 541 F.2d 1352 (9th Cir. 1976).

Page 76

Continental TV, Inc. v. GTE Sylvania, Inc., 433 U.S. 36 (1977).

Page 78

Jefferson Parish Hospital District No. 2 v. Hyde, 466 U.S. 2 (1984).

Page 79

Jefferson Parish Hospital District No. 2 v. Hyde, 466 U.S. 2 (1984).

Northern Pacific Railway v. United States, 356 U.S. 1 (1958).

Page 80

United States v. Jerrold Electronics Corp., 187 F. Supp. 545 (E.D. Pa. 1960).

Baker v. Simmons Co., 307 F.2d 458 (1st Cir. 1962).

Krehl v. Baskin-Robbins Ice Cream Co., 664 F.2d 1348 (9th Cir. 1982).

United States v. Microsoft Corp., 2001-1 Trade Cases (CCH) ¶ 73,321 (D.C. Cir. 2001).

Page 81

Tampa Electric Co. v. Nashville Coal Co., 365 U.S. 320 (1961).

Page 82

Bruce's Juices, Inc. v. American Can Co., 330 U.S. 743 (1947).

Falls City Industries v. Vanco Beverage, Inc., 460 U.S. 428 (1983).

Page 88

Atari Games Corp. v. Nintendo of America, Inc., 897 F.2d 1572, 1576 (Fed. Cir. 1990).

International Salt Co. v. United States, 332 U.S. 392 (1947).

Page 95

Kobe, Inc. v. Dempsey Pump Co., 198 F.2d 416 (10th Cir. 1952).

Walker Process Equipment, Inc. v. Food Machinery & Chemical Corp., 382 U.S. 172 (1965).

Rex Chainbelt Inc. v. Harco Products, Inc., 512 F.2d 993 (9th Cir. 1975).

Page 96

Zenith Electronics Corp. v. Exzec Inc., 182 F.3d 1340, 1355 (Fed. Cir. 1999).

Professional Real Estate Investors, Inc. v. Columbia Pictures Industries, Inc., 508 U.S. 49 (1993).

Page 99

In the Matter of Intel Corp., FTC Dkt. No. 9228 (filed June 8, 1998), Consent Order (August 6, 1999).

Page 102

Zenith Radio Corp. v. Hazeltine Research, Inc., 395 U.S. 100 (1969).

United States v. General Electric Co., 272 U.S. 476 (1926).

Page 105

United States v. Microsoft Corp., 2001-1 Trade Cases (CCH) ¶ 73,321 (D.C. Cir. 2001).

Page 112

Associated General Contractors, Inc. v. California State Council of Carpenters, 459 U.S. 519 (1983).

Brunswick Corp. v. Pueblo Bowl-O-Mat, Inc., 429 U.S. 477 (1977).

Page 113

Matsushita Electric Industries Co. v. Zenith Radio Corp., 475 U.S. 574 (1986).

Page 118

Timberlane Lumber Co. v. Bank of America, 549 F.2d 597 (9th Cir. 1976).

Page 135

United States v. Microsoft Corp., 1995-2 Trade Cases (CCH) ¶ 71,096 (D.D.C. 1995).

United States v. Kanzai Specialty Papers, Inc., 6 Trade Reg. Rep. (CCH) ¶ 45,094 (D. Mass. 1994).

Index

INDEX

About the Authors

John H. Shenefield is an antitrust lawyer with the law firm of Morgan, Lewis & Bockius and is a senior partner in the firm's Antitrust and Trade Regulation Section. He is the author of numerous articles on antitrust law and competition policy and speaks frequently at seminars and symposiums on those subjects.

Mr. Shenefield received his bachelor's and law degrees from Harvard University. He was assistant attorney general in charge of the Antitrust Division of the U.S. Department of Justice from 1977 until 1980 and associate attorney general of the United States from 1979 until 1981. In addition, he was the chairman of the President's National Commission for the Review of Antitrust Laws and Procedures. He has taught antitrust courses both at the University of Richmond Law School and at Georgetown University Law School.

Irwin M. Stelzer received his bachelor's and master's degrees from New York University and his Ph.D. degree from Cornell University. He has been director of the Energy and Environmental Policy Center at

Harvard University, an associate member of Nuffield College, Oxford, a member of the Advisory Panel of the President's National Commission for the Review of Antitrust Laws and Procedures, and a scholar at the American Enterprise Institute. In addition to serving as director of regulatory studies at the Hudson Institute, Mr. Stelzer is a member of the board of the Regulatory Policy Institute, Oxford, and a political and economic columnist for the *Sunday Times* (London) and the *New York Post*.